ELECTIONS IN
NIGERIA

A GRASSROOTS PERSPECTIVE

WILLIAM MILES

ELECTIONS IN NIGERIA

A GRASSROOTS PERSPECTIVE

LYNNE RIENNER PUBLISHERS
BOULDER & LONDON

Photographs by William Miles,
unless otherwise stated

Published in the United States of America in 1988 by
Lynne Rienner Publishers, Inc.
948 North Street, Boulder, Colorado 80302

and in the United Kingdom by
Lynne Rienner Publishers, Inc.
3 Henrietta Street, Covent Garden, London WC2E 8LU

Library of Congress Cataloging-in-Publication Data

Miles, William F. S.
  Elections in Nigeria.

  Bibliography: p.
  Includes index.
   1. Elections—Nigeria, Northern—Case studies.
2. Political participation—Nigeria, Northern—Case
studies. 3. Hausas—Political activity—Case studies.
JQ3099.N66E546 1987   324.9669'505   87-16790
ISBN 1-55587-054-6

Printed and bound in the United States of America

The paper used in this publication meets the
requirements of the American National Standard
for Permanence of Paper for Printed Library
Materials Z39.48-1984. ∞

Pour Loïza,
Princesse de Yardaji

Contents

Illustrations

MAPS

FIGURES

TABLES

Preface

Nigeria's New Year's coup d'état of 1984 effectively invalidated the results of that country's previous elections, held in the summer of 1983. The 1983 elections— fraught with bribery, ballot-stuffing, violence, and uncountable instances of corruption— were themselves invoked as a cause of, and legitimization for, the military's toppling of Shehu Shagari's civilian regime. The full story of the 1983 Nigerian elections has yet to be told, although the chapter seems to be closed— at least for now— on Africa's most significant "democratic experiment."

Nevertheless, even if the 1983 vote no longer holds any legitimacy in Nigeria itself, great light has been shed on the attempt, however flawed, to extend the electoral process on a significant scale to a Third World setting. Larry Diamond[1] and Richard Joseph[2] have given us a glimpse of what the "democratic experiment" has meant (or done) to Nigeria on the national level. Further, "macro" level studies of Nigeria's Second Republic may be anticipated, and should be welcomed.

Broad-based, nation-wide examinations of African elections are of course invaluable, and contribute immensely to the study of politics in the developing world. Nevertheless, the political scientist's classical approach to studying electoral behavior (i.e., interviewing high-level candidates, inspecting party platforms, analyzing electoral results) may obscure more indigenous, culturally relevant implications of the democratic process in non-western contexts. Indeed, while providing a necessary heuristic framework for western understanding of democratic experiments in the Third World, they do not necessarily tell us how members of those cultures themselves perceive, interpret, and conceptualize these same phenomena.

Traditionally, western analyses of African, and particularly Nigerian, politics have been unabashedly elite-oriented. Just as the movement for African nationalism and decolonization was viewed as a phenomenon spearheaded by the westernized African elite, so were post-independence African politics also regarded as the *chasse gardée* of this same upper class of sophisticated "New Africans." As an example, we may cite the admission (and omission) from the otherwise insightful work of Kenneth Post and Michael Vickers, in their study of structure and conflict in Nigerian First Republic politics and elections:

> [T]his is to a large extent a study of political elites; although at certain points it raises the question of mass political behavior, it does not take this as its prime focus. Given the nature of the Nigerian political system under the First Republic, where the mass of the population were regarded by the elite as objects of manipulation rather than real participants, we feel this emphasis to be justified.[3]

While not addressing herself to any one study in particular, Margaret Peil exposes the ramifications of this tendency of conventional political scientists and commentators to bypass the vast majority of Africans (and Nigerians) in their analyses:

> The result of this concentration on the elites is a disdain for the general public which can be a serious hindrance to the accurate analysis of political events. Both local elites and foreigners seem to believe that the people are not really important, that plans made "for the common good" will eventually be appreciated, that public behavior is often irrational and must be controlled, that people are ignorant and uninterested in their national government and should be discouraged from interfering.[4]

Elite-bias in Africanist political science does not result merely in partial analysis, incomplete understanding, or unfortunate oversight; Peil claims that there is a more insidious process operating as well: "These writers seldom consider that the elites, who supply the information, intend at all costs to maintain their power, prestige and perquisites . . . and that ordinary citizens may prefer to pick and choose their way through the alternatives."[5]

Peil made this critique, and wrote her book on Nigerian public opinion, in the military interregnum between the First and Second republics. The present work aims to incorporate Peil's "people's view" perspective in the context of Nigeria's more recent bout with democratic and electoral politics.

The purpose of this book is to present a case study of what the electoral process in Nigeria has meant, both on a "micro" level and in culturally specific terms. The scale of perspective is that of a single rural village and its outlying district; the psychocultural context (or *Weltanschauung*) is that of the Hausa people. Based on formal interviews and informal discussions with local party candidates and leaders, attendance at local political rallies, observation of actual voting and tabulation, and general participation in the daily lives of rural villagers before, during, and after the campaign itself, the book provides an anthropological perspective to the political scientist's domain. While in no way claiming that the conclusions are valid for other cultural groups in rural Africa, or even throughout Nigeria, it nevertheless offers a living portrait of how western modes of democracy may "trickle down" to a Third World village level, and how the anthropological approach may be invoked to enhance the methodology of political science. Although it encompasses aspects of political anthropology, it also transcends it. For while political anthropologists generally study indigenous political structures and processes in small-scale communities, the present study examines the functioning of a strictly western or "modern" system of government in a non-western cultural environment. In short, the study tries to explain what Nigerian democracy has meant through Hausa eyes.

Acknowledgments

What you are holding in your hands is the product of sheer Felicity. When I departed for Nigeria in February of 1983, I had no intention of conducting an electoral study of any nature, and was only dimly aware of that country's scheduled elections six months away. I went to Nigeria, and settled in Yardaji on the Northern frontier, with the aim of conducting a comparative study of two neighboring Hausa villages in Nigeria and Niger. The campaign and elections slowly and naturally unfolded as part of village life on the Nigerian side of the border. I had not come to Yardaji to observe elections or politics in that village; rather, Yardaji came to educate *me* in Nigerian elections and politics.

There is something to be said for this kind of unintended, evolving research agenda. For one thing, it helps ensure that the researcher's focus is not an exaggeration or overblown version of the phenomenon that he is observing and investigating. I had no scholarly *need*, or even predisposition, to write a book on Nigeria's and Yardaji's elections; I believe that this circumstance alone has enabled me to keep the following study in its proper perspective. Second, by allowing one's research agenda to emerge naturally, one is less prejudiced by preconceived paradigms, less inclined to prove (or defend) predetermined hypotheses, and less driven to corroborate (or refute) the prevailing literature. In short, one's mind-set is fresher and, although it is a risky claim to make in any social science endeavor, one's approach is all the more "objective." Just as I "happened" to be in Martinique in 1981 when France voted in François Mitterrand and a Socialist govern-

15

ment—which became the springboard for my first book—so did I "happen" to be in Yardaji in 1983 when Shehu Shagari and his NPN government were returned to power. I was also in Yardaji when Shagari was arrested by the military, the constitution suspended, the borders closed, and the Second Republic relegated to history. (Until the Nigerian radio began broadcasting this news in Hausa, I was also, thanks to the BBC and Voice of America, one of the few sources of village information on these events.) I finally left Nigeria in late January of 1984; and while not all of that year was as dramatic as the election campaign and the coup, it was a year of constant challenge and learning. For that year, I must thank the Fulbright Research Program.

While in Nigeria I was affiliated, as research associate, with Bayero University in Kano. M. K. Bashir, then acting head of the Department of Sociology, helped facilitate the affiliation. Also at BUK, Drs. Abdel Muta'al zein el Abdin Ahmed, Momodou Darboe, Larry Diamond, Ali Farbood, Martin Fisher, Shahina Ghazanfar, Gerry Kleis, and Michael Mortimore were all responsible for my survival in Kano. For permission to conduct research in their state, I must also thank the authorities of Kaduna state. In Daura, His Royal Highness Alhaji Muhammadu Bashar extended and exemplified the hospitality for which his emirate is so well known. At the emir's palace, Alhaji Sani, Yahaya Yusufu, Alhaji Idi Salihu, Ubandawaki, and all the other *dogarai* must be greeted with thanks. Alhajis Lawal and Galadima also made my visits to Daura so pleasant and rewarding. And without Gambo Mai-Mai's help in Zango, how would I ever have made it to Daura as I did?

It is to the people of Yardaji, *duk jama'a gaba daya*, to whom I owe my greatest *godiya*. First and foremost is Yardaji's chief (Sarkin Fulani), Alhaji Harou. Accepting me, in customary Hausa fashion, as a *bako*, he personified the generosity and hospitality that the entire village extended me. His sons, Hassan and Ibrahim, must be mentioned for the same reason.

Sarkin Zabe ("King of the Elections") Lawal Nuhu was, and remains, an incomparable friend and helper. Sani Dauda ("Iresco") kept me mobile on the Honda, just as Mamman took such great care of Wahalla, my indefatigable mount. Alhaji Usman, Alhaji Musa Tela, Alhaji Lassan, Alhaji Kosso, Alhaji Ali (and his son, Moutari), Ousseini, Sidi, Malam Ja, Ilu, Taigaza, and Issaka (Sarkin Rawa) all made my stay in Yardaji a joy. Space alone prevents me from acknowledging the others.

In a sense, none of this would have happened were it not for the Peace Corps. As a volunteer in Niger (1977–1979), I not only achieved fluency in the Hausa language but gained an immense respect for (and a humble understanding of) Hausa life and culture. The person who guided me in my initial journey into Hausaland, and who led me—both literally and figuratively—from Magaria to Yardaji, is Mallam Souleymane Abdou dan Tata.

To all of these friends I must say *Na gode*; for any errors or omissions, I will say *Na tuba.*

Professors Naomi Chazan and Dov Ronen, at the Africa Research Program at Harvard University, encouraged me to present and publish my findings. For the maps and figures, I must thank my research assistants at Northeastern University, Mr. Mahfuzal Chowdhury, Mr. Yotin Padungton, and Ms. Laurie Weinstein.

"Main Street" in Yardaji

Introduction

On Saturday, August 6, 1983, the inhabitants of Yardaji, an insignificant Hausa village on the northern outskirts of Kaduna state— a minuscule constituency in the African mammoth that is Nigeria— found themselves directly linked to the Federal Republic in a most dramatic way. For on that day, Yardaji-ites voted, along with twenty-five million other Nigerians, for the man they hoped would be their nation's head of state for the next four years. Four successive Saturdays would see the villagers voting for their state governor, federal senator, federal house representative, and state assembly representative; it was only in the presidential contest, however, that Yardaji was faced with a choice identical to that of the entire Nigerian electorate.

Yardaji joined Nigeria's absolute majority in reelecting the nation's incumbent president, Alhaji Shehu Shagari, and affirming his ruling National Party of Nigeria (NPN). In pluralistic Nigeria, long beset by ethnic, regional, and religious rivalry, such an outcome is hardly surprising: Shagari, like Yardaji, was Northern, Muslim, Hausa, and— like Yardaji's own village chief— of Fulani background. And, many might have argued, it is only natural that Yardaji-ites— uneducated, illiterate peasant farmers— would unanimously back the one national political figure who best epitomized their own sociocultural profile and with whom they could most readily identify.

Unfortunately, this simplistic image of a politically unsophisticated rural African electorate, motivated or manipulated by purely "tribal" considerations, is one fostered by various groups.

19

One consists of a portion of the continent's own elites, who take the quiescent "bush" for granted, looking invariably to the city as a source of national potential, intellectual interest, or personal advantage. There exists as well a certain class of western political scientists for whom Third World politics has simply become a matter of "ethnic arithmetic." While electoral analysis of urban, pluralistic, and cosmopolitan populations is considered a worthwhile and legitimate undertaking, it is assumed in advance that rural, ethnically homogeneous communities will vote as a block, to "protect" themselves from foreign (i.e., ethnically dissimilar) influence and/or rulers.

The case of Yardaji's participation in the Nigerian elections in the summer of 1983 belies these preconceptions. Political activity in the village was far from passive, and had little to do with "tribal" fears, suasion, or demagogy. In fact, even in this impoverished rural community, where every adult knows one another, speaks the same language, practices the same religion, survives by virtue of a technologically primitive, near-subsistence agriculture— even here, in the archetypical Sahelian bush, every Nigerian party, of every ethnic and ideological imprimatur, scored points.

At the same time, village support for the various parties— as reflected in the ultimate distribution of votes— should not be misconstrued to indicate the villagers' support for the *system* of politics *per se*. For if any one theme should be singled out from the following narration of Yardaji's participation in the Nigerian elections of 1983, it is that Yardaji-ites came not only to take a negative attitude toward civilian politics as a process but also to assume a jaded view of electoral democracy as an idea. To understand *why* and *how* they came to this position, however, it is not sufficient to merely recount or document the corruption and collapse of Nigerian politics in the Second Republic; it is at least as necessary to understand the inner workings of Hausa— or at least rural Hausa— life, thought, and culture.

CHAPTER ONE

The Setting

In the sandy, flat, arid expanse of the Sahel—where rain falls ("if God is willing") only three months out of the year—lies the village of Yardaji. Tucked away in the northeastern panhandle of Kaduna state, a scant mile from the border with the Republic of Niger, Yardaji is hardly a recognizable place name for either specialists or inhabitants of greater Northern Nigeria. Although the official population (according to government census) is over six thousand, the true population is closer to four thousand. Within the larger context of Nigeria (whose population ranges between eighty and one-hundred-twenty million), Yardaji represents no more than a needle in the demographic haystack of the country. (See the map, "Yardaji in Nigeria.")

By Nigerian standards, Yardaji is poor. Most people live in square mud huts, with mud-and-thatch roofs that must be reinforced before the annual rainy season to prevent leakage. (In recent years, some of the wealthier inhabitants have built cement huts with aluminum "pan" roofs.) There is no electricity, no running water: two hand-cranked pumps and wells dispersed throughout the village supply water; kerosene lamps and flashlights offer specks of illumination after dark. Health care and sanitary conditions are barely existent; despite a dispensary building and its supervising attendant, disease prevention is practically nil, and infants die regularly. Even in such conditions, however, the people are conscious of their relative prosperity: Yardaji-ites look down upon their "truly" poor neighbors across the border in Niger, who live in grass (instead of mud) huts and travel exclusively by donkey, horse, or foot. (There are dozens of bicycles and twenty motorcycles in Yardaji, and the village is serviced, however erratically, by market-linking minibuses.)

The villagers' economy (and survival) basically revolves around a single activity: rain-fed grain agriculture, particularly of millet and sorghum, the staples of the community's diet. In addition, there is a significant degree of livestock raising: goats, sheep, cattle. Since the annual agricultural season comprises only a portion of the calendar year (from soil preparation in May to harvest in September), many Yardaji-ites have secondary occupations as well: men may be carpenters, butchers, smiths, potters, and tailors, and women commercial meal and snack sellers. There are two elementary schools on each side of the village, but children are more greatly appreciated for their contribution to their family's farming activities. (Households generally possess a number of small plots— a couple of acres or so— scattered haphazardly in various directions and distances from the village.)

Virtually all of the inhabitants of Yardaji are Hausa, although some (four households, including the chief's family) are of Fulani descent. Hausas are renowned sedentary, agricultural, town and village dwellers; the Fulanis' prowess lies in their nomadic and

Yardaji in Nigeria

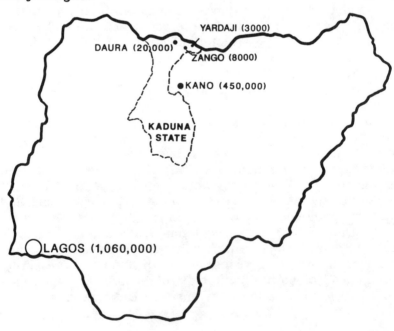

seminomadic livestock raising. Accordingly, the latter reside in small, mobile, single-family camps or settlements. Many such Fulani camps dot the sparse countryside around Yardaji. Although the "urbanized," "sophisticated" Hausa (as even Yardaji-ites see themselves) revel in good-naturedly mocking the more "backward" Fulani "bushmen," in and around Yardaji the Hausa and Fulani generally are on excellent terms with one another. (The fact that the Yardaji chief himself has roots in one of these nearby Fulani settlements helps to strengthen local Hausa-Fulani ties.) Both groups practice Islam, and all (with the exception of some Fulani females) speak Hausa, the *lingua franca* of the over twenty million persons throughout Northern Nigeria. (Fulanis can also speak Fulfulde, their native tongue; relatively few individuals in the Northern Nigerian countryside can communicate in English.)

ADMINISTRATIVE STRUCTURE

In Hausaland, the smallest settlement is called *gari*, or village, and is headed by the village chief (*mai-gari*). With around four thousand inhabitants, Yardaji constitutes a *gunduma*, or village area, encompassing Yardaji village proper, along with seven smaller, outlying villages (Bulungudu, Kututure, Kanda, Jawo, Gadawo, Dichi, and Mai-Zabo). Thus the *mai-gari* of Yardaji is also the *dagaci*, or village area head, for the entire Yardaji area.

Yardaji village area falls within the district (*karamin hukuma*) of Zango, which contains fourteen other village areas besides Yardaji. The *hakimi* (district head) has traditional jurisdiction over the entire district, but shares responsibility with the *kantoma* (local government administrator). The *kantoma* is a relatively new position instituted by the state, without precedent in indigenous Hausa government.[1]

Zango is actually only one of five district areas within the emirate of Daura. (The others are Daura itself, Maiadua, Sandamu, and Baure; see the map, "Yardaji in Daura.") The emirate is presided over by the *sarki*, or emir, who, in the case of Daura, gains immense prestige by virtue of the fact that Daura is traditionally considered the birthplace of the entire Hausa nation, going back several thousand years. Depending on the position, traditional leaders are selected by different procedures, although these invariably combine democratic with hereditary criteria. Thus, while the choice of emir is made by the traditional king-

Yardaji in Daura

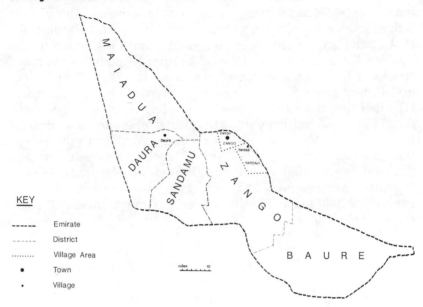

maker's council, and ratified by the state, district and village heads are appointed by the emir and his council (but must be from their predecessor's family). Village chiefs, in contrast, are popularly elected by the villagers themselves.

Kaduna state, in which Daura emirate, Zango district, and Yardaji village and village area lie, contains seven emirates and seventy local government areas. (Kaduna itself is but one of nineteen states throughout the Federal Republic of Nigeria.) Thus, Yardaji represents a fairly ordinary, relatively insignificant community within a much grander scheme of Nigerian politics and administration. (See the figure, "Administrative Structure.")

PRE-COUP NIGERIA

At the time of the 1983 elections (and since 1979), the Nigerian government was patterned after that of the United States Constitution. A president (in Hausa, *shugaban kasa*, or "leader of the nation") and vice-president (*mai-taimakon shugaban kasa*, the "president's helper") were elected for renewable four-year terms. The federal legislative body was composed of a Senate (ninety-five members) as well as a House of Representatives (four-hundred-fifty members). Each state had a single legislative chamber (the House of Assembly, which, in Kaduna state, was composed of ninety-nine members [*wakilai*]). The state executive, as in the United States, was the governor (*gwamna*, in anglicized Hausa).

In 1983, all elected officials were up for reelection. Thus, the voters of Yardaji— like voters throughout Nigeria— were to go to

Administrative Structure

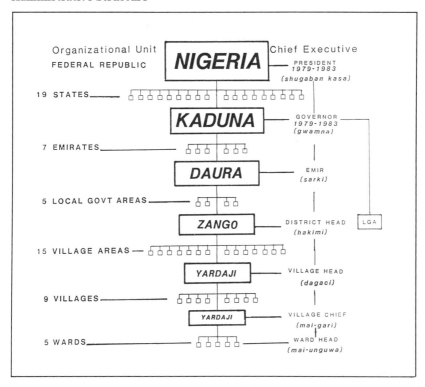

the polls in five successive weeks, to choose a president and vice-president, a governor, a federal senator, a federal house representative, and a state Assembly representative. General elections for the *kantoma* (who hitherto had been appointed) were scheduled to follow the national elections in early 1984. Following the coup, however, these elections were cancelled.

THE DUAL POLITY

It is important to stress that, for the people of Yardaji (as throughout most of Africa), there are two institutions of government operating simultaneously. These are often referred to as "traditional" and "modern," but, perhaps more accurately, should be thought of as "indigenous" and "post-colonial." In Nigeria, as in many former British colonies, the distinction between the two is often not so clear-cut, for the British, unlike the French, deliberately attempted to incorporate traditional chieftaincies within the administrative and governing structures. Even today there is a dovetailing and harmony of indigenous and post-colonial institutions in Anglophone Africa not to be found in the more dichotomized "traditional" and "modern" institutions found in former French colonies.

"Indigenous" government refers to the manner in which African communities organized themselves to carry out political functions (e.g., law and order, dispute resolution, leadership selection) prior to European conquest. It also encompasses patterns of loyalty or fealty to larger political groupings, such as emirates, kingdoms, or empires. In Yardaji, for instance, people owe traditional allegiance and respect to their particular ward-head, or *mai-unguwa* (in Yardaji there are five such wards, or neighborhoods), then village chief (*mai-gari*, who in this case is also their village area head, or *dagaci*), then the district head (*hakimi*) of Zango, and then the emir (*sarki*) of Daura. Since the Fulani conquest of Hausaland at the turn of the nineteenth century, an even higher level of loyalty has been established, to the sultan of Sokoto (*Sarkin Mussulmi*, or "King of the Muslims"). While the role and significance of indigenous, or traditional, rulers (*sarakai na gargajiya*) have changed since the colonial era, the titles themselves are firmly entrenched within Hausa history and culture, and provide a crucial, and comforting, institutional continuity alongside the more fleeting, and often turbulent, post-colonial forms of government.

Among villagers in Africa, references to the colonial era evoke a completely different response than they do amongst the educated elite, for whom "colonialism" represents an unmitigated evil. The very term "to colonize," *raino*, indicates this perspective: in Hausa it means literally "caring for, nursing." In Yardaji, this "nursing period" still connotes the lifting of ignorance (*duhu*, or "darkness") through the introduction of education and knowledge (*ilmi*). Independence (*'yanci*) has acquainted the people with two other forms of government, in addition to the indigenous and colonial ones: military regimes (*mulkin soja*, or "rule of the soldier") and civilian government (*mulkin farin fula*, literally "rule of the white hats," to distinguish begowned and bedecked politicians from bare-headed soldiers). While European colonialists, military rulers, and civilian politicians have come and gone, only the *sarakai na gargajiya*— the indigenous rulers, or chieftaincy— has prevailed throughout. And although traditional leaders have always been hierarchically subordinate to the "modern" rulers (who have exerted varying degrees of control over them), their longevity and stability confer a legitimacy in the eyes of the villagers that more powerful, but transient, colonial and post-colonial rulers have never achieved.

In general, even prior to the 1984 New Year's coup, most people in Yardaji expressed a preference for *mulkin soja*— military rule— to *mulkin farin fula*— civilian government. The extent of personal enrichment by high-level politicians in office may not have been fully known on the village level, but instances of petty graft and corruption were all too common. These ranged from shakedowns by roving police bands for alleged traffic offenses to outright payments for favorable judgments in both criminal and civil litigation. Military rule, on the other hand, was associated with many of the virtues of traditional Hausa rule, such as *iko* (authority, power) and *biyayya* (obedience). Even if harsh, rigid, or severe (as the subsequent Buhari government came to be regarded), military rule has resembled pre-colonial-style government more than civilian politics has. It thereby incarnated recognizable and familiar features and qualities to which ordinary Hausa can easily relate, submit, and, ultimately, respect.

SUMMARY

As the above discussion indicates, the concepts and terminology of comparative government institutions and political systems are firmly grounded in the culture and language of rural Hausaland. There is little correlation between technological and political sophistication: the villagers of Yardaji, despite a life of material hardship, bring a rich vocabulary and keen interest to the subjects of politics, government, and administration. Four kinds of regimes can be distinguished from one another: indigenous (*gargajiya*), colonial (*raino*), military (*soja*), and civilian (*farin fula*). Two structures of administration exist simultaneously: a traditional one, linking villages *(garuruwa)* to districts within emirates *(kasashe)*; and a modern one, composed of local government areas and states *(jihohi)*. Finally, the dual polity entails parallel personnel hierarchies, consisting of chiefs and emirs *(masu-gari, hakimai, sarakuna)* on the one hand, and— at least from 1979 to 1984— representatives, governors, and presidents *(wakilai, gwamnoni, shugabanni-kasa)* on the other. Far from resulting in any undue complexity or confusion, however, Yardaji-ites are astonished to hear that a country (such as the author's) can function on the basis of "modern" political institutions alone. For them, it is the idea of a society functioning *without* a chieftaincy, in fact, which verges on the incredible.

CHAPTER TWO

The "Democratization" of Daura

POLITICS IN NORTHERN NIGERIA

Nineteen eighty-three may have presented the most recent opportunity for the inhabitants of Yardaji to participate in electoral and partisan politics, but it was hardly the first time that they were exposed to such phenomena. The principle of popular election had been introduced into Northern Nigeria over two decades prior, in 1951, while the country was still under British rule. "Guided democracy" and "gradualism" (the latter term is C. S. Whitaker's) under the British was a far cry, of course, from the no-holds-barred, free-for-all scramble that politics became under the Second Republic. Nevertheless, the various attempts to "modernize" and "democratize" the Nigerian (and hence Hausa) polity ever since the end of the Second World War may be regarded as critical rehearsals for the 1983 drama. Given that the constitution of the Second Republic was designed to eliminate the flaws and defects of previous democratic designs in Nigeria, it is important to review what those previous attempts at democratization had given way to. Fortunately, invaluable previous studies have examined the original introduction of western democratic norms and structures not only to Northern Nigeria in general but to Yardaji's own district—the emirate of Daura—in particular.[1]

In 1903, British rule was effectively extended over Nigerian Hausaland when British military forces defeated the sultan of Sokoto at the battle of Burmi. Unlike the French, for whom colonialism in African entailed the policies of Direct Rule and *as-*

similation (the extension of French cultural norms and administrative structures to colonial subjects), British colonial rule, as
formulated by Sir Frederick Lugard, had a more *laissez-faire*
quality about it. For Indirect Rule, as it was to be called, entailed
the retention of the pre-colonial forms of government (i.e., the Fulani emirate system) in an attempt to gradually encourage the
evolution of the Hausa political culture and system toward the
British mold. Crucially, this was to be done within the more familiar (and theoretically less disruptive) framework of indigenous
rule.

Some British felt an innate empathy for the Hausa system of
government, which paralleled, they believed, Britain's own history of constitutional monarchy, political and social stratification, and empire building. Unlike the peoples of southern Nigeria
with whom they had had previous contact (especially the Igbo
and the Yoruba), the British found among the Hausa a structure
with which they could identify: one characterized by strong
leadership, centralized government, and established religion. Official British policy was thus to accept, entrench, and relegitimize
the prevailing "religio-political orthodoxy."[2] Islam was accorded
the status of "native law and custom" and, with a view toward
protecting the Islamic integrity of the North, laws were passed
severely restricting Christian missionary activity.

Indirect Rule was nevertheless fundamentally ambivalent.
On the one hand, British colonial philosophy was to effectuate
change and progress, and eventually to introduce a system of
participatory democracy. On the other hand, the British wished
to preserve the stability and order that pre-colonial rule engendered, reasoning that only inefficiency (if not social anarchy)
would follow radical and rapid change. The somewhat paradoxi-
cal policy was to "induce fundamental change within the boundaries of the established political order."[3] Not surprisingly, "the
resulting political system reflected normative ambiguity and am-
bivalence."[4]

The legal framework through which Indirect Rule was to be
implemented was the Native Authorities Ordinance. Originally
promulgated in 1933, the legislation regarding the "NAs" was re-
vised in 1943 and then frequently throughout the 1950s. Originally, the traditional emirs were designated as "sole native
authorities"; that is, they were recognized as the executive em-
bodiments of the local NA administrations. Law and order, public works, sanitation and health, agriculture and forestry (along
with other local government services) were thus overseen by the

traditional rulers and technically subject to the mere "advice" of the British colonial residents. Eventually (although this varied by emirate), the emirs were transformed from sole native authorities to chiefs-in-council and, in some cases, chiefs-and-council. The purpose of these reforms was to create a degree of executive accountability for the emirs, governing now, according to principle, only with the support and consent of their local councils. Yet the overriding influence and power of the emirs was only slightly mitigated, if at all, by these reforms; one account calls this a change from aristocracy to, not democracy, but a "modernizing oligarchy."[5] Another account (focusing specifically on the Daura emirate) refers to it as "a patrimonial regime under British supervision."[6]

One factor invoked to explain the continuing dominance of the chieftaincy despite local government reform, and despite the subsequent attempts to extend popular participation through the electoral system, is the phenomenon of clientship. Hausa political culture, no less than Hausa society in general, is bound up in the mutual dependence of superiors and subordinates. In Hausa political terms, this entails the responsibility of the *sarakuna*, the rulers, for the welfare of their client commoners, the *talakawa*; conversely, clientage demands the loyalty of the *talakawa* vis-à-vis their patron *sarakuna*. More specifically, traditional leadership is seen to rest on the three social pegs of stratification, hereditary legitimacy, and personalism.[7] The earliest attempts to democratize Nigerian Hausaland— at least to seriously democratize it, in the western sense of popular participation and political equality— necessarily ran afoul of these indigenous norms of Hausa political culture. Reform of the *structure* of government, on both the local and regional levels (bureaucratic, parliamentary, and councilor) led to cooptation of the new structures by the *sarakuna*. The creation of a party system of politics and political competition led to similar results.

Beginning in the postwar phase of colonial rule, and continuing throughout Nigeria's First Republic (1960–1966), competitive politics in the North became a contest, however lopsided, between two parties. The Northern People's Congress (NPC, or *Jamiyyar MutanenArewa* in Hausa) dominated the Northern Elements Progressive Union (NEPU, or *Jamiyyar Neman Sawaba*). By extension, it dominated all political activity in the Northern region of Nigeria. As a consequence, the principle of clientage, the supremacy of the *sarakuna*, and the continuity of tradition all survived the western intrusions of partisan politics and electoral democracy.

The goal of the Northern People's Congress was to "combine traditionalism with moderate but progressive reform."[8] Its central objectives were as follows: regional autonomy within a united Nigeria; local government reform within a progressive emirate system; retention of the traditional selection of emirs; furtherance of education, with respect for indigenous culture; self-governance within the commonwealth; one North, one people.

Pre-colonial and colonial elites and institutions provided both the leadership and form of the NPC. The sardauna of Sokoto and the emir of Katsina became leaders of the party, which was in turn supported by village and district heads, NA civil servants, western-educated elites, prosperous merchants, and the highest levels of the chieftaincy. (This latter basis of support belied the "myth of neutrality," i.e., that the *sarakuna*, as quasi-constitutional monarchs, would and could remain above the fray of partisan and competitive politics.) The NPC's ties with the chiefs was the most problematic, for it needed their support if it hoped to get *talakawa* votes. (On voting no less than on other matters, the *talakawa* looked to their traditional leaders for advice and leadership.) On the other hand, the NPC needed to assert its hegemony over the chieftaincy if it wished to be independent of it. In the end, a mutually rewarding, if not intimate, relationship was struck up between the two parties and traditional institutions.

Administratively, the party was divided according to the emirate structure, and paralleled the Native Authorities' jurisdictions. The NPC local party chairman, for instance, was more likely than not to be the NA district head. But whereas the NPC succeeded in reinforcing itself through its identification with these known and familiar bureaucracies, its hierarchical nature minimized true interaction with low-level party members and feedback to party elites. The NPC was "a weakly articulated, organizationally diffuse, but highly centralized political party."[9]

The NPC emphasized its link with the past, and its ties to Islam. Its emblem was a green flag, the same symbol that the Fulani Usman dan Fodio used during his Islamicizing *jihad* in the early nineteenth century. Not only did Ahmadu Bello, the NPC president-general and *sardauna* of Sokoto, stress that he was the great-grandson of Usman, but he called himself Bayajidda II (after the mythical founder of the Seven Hausa Families in Daura), and even claimed direct descent from Mohammed himself. Bello's annual pilgrimage to Mecca, although considered extravagant by some, was used to reinforce the connection between the NPC and Islam.

Islam itself promotes social consensus as a fundamental tenet of the faith: patriotism and party unity were likewise extended religious overtones. The trinity of party, faith, and community was awarded the status of *ijma*– social consensus– and an opponent to any of these was by definition *bidi'a*– a rebel from the community. Thus, while the form of political collectivity– the party– was "modern," its content– political consensus through religious unity– merely replicated the results of the Fulani *jihad*.

As mentioned above, the NPC assimilated the familiar clientage institution into its procedures. The nature of the rewards may have altered (e.g., job patronage, loans, scholarships, contracts), but the nature of the superior-subordinate link through gift and service exchange did not change. In the process, the pattern of hierarchical dependence was applied to the party structure.

The party system, at least as represented by the NPC, did not operate for the benefit of the lowly, if majoritarian, *talakawa*. Within the NPC itself there was virtually no input from the peasant class; they simply received party directives and acted accordingly. The advent of parliamentary elections did little to change the long-established relationship between *sarakuna* and *talakawa*, the rulers and the ruled, the leaders and the followers. "The Northern People's Congress is not a political party [but] merely a political expression for an existing system of administration dyed in religion and innate tradition," declared an opposition newspaper.[10]

The Northern Elements Progressive Union, in contrast, had the *talakawa* as its very focus, and wished to radically transform Hausaland into an egalitarian society. Led by the populist firebrand Mallam Aminu Kano, NEPU took aim at the "corrupt and degenerate" chieftaincy, whose vested interests and privileges it declared intolerable. It was "dedicated to the 'emancipation of the *talakawa* from domination by these privileged few' through 'reform of the present autocratic political institutions.'"[11] Support for NEPU came from disaffected nobles (who had failed to achieve office under the NA/NPC administration), independent traders (who had little political status in pre-colonial society), and *'yan iska* (literally "sons of the wind")– urban youth, with no acceptable social role or steady occupation.

NEPU tried to exploit potential resentment on the part of the *Habes*– the "pure" Hausa indigenes– against the ruling Fulanis, who had governed the emirates ever since the *jihad* of Usman dan Fodio. (Fulani emirs had replaced the Hausa *sarakuna*, and their dynasties came to constitute a major part of the aristocracy of Hausaland.) But unlike many African regions, where ethnic differentiation and rivalry are often explosive, the situation in Hausaland is less volatile. Over the years, through intermarriage and cultural assimilation, the once-conquering Fulanis have adopted the language and customs of their post-*jihad* subjects. (Many such *Filanin gida*, or "town-Fulanis," no longer speak Fulfulde, the Fulani language.) Fulanis *are* part of Hausa society; hence the common ethnic amalgamatory term "Hausa-Fulani." At the same time, the descendants of the *Habes* have unambiguously embraced Islam, creating that higher level of unity that transcends supposed ethnic differentiation.

Still, NEPU attempted to install new values and sentiments by reference to a pre-Fulani epoch of Hausa history. It also attempted to distinguish the original Fulani *jihadists* from their more decadent descendants, and to link the original Fulani revolution with NEPU's own reformist aims. Thus Usman dan Fodio and his brother Abdullahi were considered "great Moslem democrats," who, like NEPU, wished to purify a corrupted society.[12]

NEPU did not see itself as threatening tradition. Rather, it believed it was restoring, reinvigorating, and relegitimizing the original tenets of social revolutionary Islam. Programmatically, its platform was *Girman-Ubangiji, Gama-Kai, Taimakon-Jama'a*— to praise God, to unite in self-help, and to serve the community. As with the NPC, NEPU settled on symbols that would foster its own links with Islam, particularly the star (from the star and crescent). It identified with the reformist, puritanical, and missionary Tijaniyya branch of West African Islam, as opposed to the more conservative (and Sokoto Fulani-affiliated) Qadariyya branch. Unlike the regionalist NPC, the nationalist NEPU called for "one Nigeria," invoking the Koran's tolerance for Christians, Jews, and religious minorities as legitimation for cross-cultural, cross-sectoral, and cross-regional unity. It was in this spirit that NEPU entered into a pact with the southern (and particularly Igbo) National Council of Nigerian Citizens (NCNC), led by Dr. Nnamdi Azikiwe. (The other major Nigerian party of the First Republic, the Action Group led by [the Yoruba] Chief Obafemi Awolowo, did contest elections in the North, but made little headway there.)

But NEPU never did succeed in mobilizing the *talakawa* masses to its call throughout Northern Nigeria. For one thing, the *talakawa* had no reason to believe that NEPU could win, and were hence unwilling to risk whatever clientelistic-derived security and protection they already had. In the face of an ancient hierarchical stratification and centralized form of government, minor political inroads were worthless (and perhaps risky), and sudden, major ones were impossible. In addition, convincing the *Habes* that they were dominated by the Fulanis had limited potential, since the system had always permitted—via entrepreneurial activity, marriage, and achievement-earned office (*shigege*)—an irreducible degree of social mobility on the part of the *Habes*. In addition, in Hausaland the unifying strength of Islam far overweighed the potentially divisive force of ethnicity.

With the ballot, then, the peasantry continued to demonstrate the same deference toward traditional leadership as it had prior to the introduction of electoral politics.[13] Direct voting and the secret ballot did little to enhance NEPU's relative electoral strength. In fact, in the ten-year span during which regional elections under party banners were contested (1954–1964), the margin of NPC dominance progressively *increased.* (See Table 2.1.)

Table 2.1   Results of Northern Nigerian Elections
             (Colonial Era and First Republic)

Election	Number of Constituencies Won			
	NPC	NEPU	Action Group	Other
1954	79	--	1	10
1956	107	9	4	11
1959	134	8	25	7
1961	156	1	9	--
1964	162	4		1

Source: C. S. Whitaker, The Politics of Tradition: Continuity
          and Change in Northern Nigeria 1946-1966 (Princeton:
          Princeton University Press, 1970): 374.

FOCUS ON DAURA

The name "Yardaji" will strike few responsive chords, even among specialists of Northern Nigeria. Yet the emirate of "Daura," within whose ambit Yardaji is squarely planted, is well-known to students of Hausa history and the subsequent creation of British Nigeria. For, according to indigenous mythology, Daura is considered the birthplace of the founding Seven Families (*Hausa Bakwai*), and hence the cradle of Hausa civilization.

According to legend, a certain Persian prince, Bayajidda, came to the city of Daura during his wanderings from Baghdad. At that time (ten, twenty centuries ago?), Daura may have been a matrifocal society, inasmuch as its previous rulers had always been queens.

Daura was plagued by a snake which, except on Fridays, prohibited access to the Kusugu town well. The fearless Bayajidda insisted on drawing water anyway, and decapitated the snake when challenged by it. As recompense, the queen of Daura offered Bayajidda half of her town. Bayajidda demurred, preferring the queen herself as his prize. Thus were Bayajidda and Daura joined in marriage. Their son, Bawo, and Bawo's own six sons were to become the kings of the seven original Hausa states: Daura, Kano, Katsina, Zaria, Gobir, Rano, and Biram.[14]

The historical accuracy of the Bayajidda legend is of course subject to academic debate. In modern-day Hausaland, however, Daura's claim to Hausa primogeniture goes unchallenged. This is so despite Daura's subsequent eclipse by the larger Hausa emirates of Kano and Katsina, and the rise of the Sokoto Hausa-Fulani state and empire.[15]

In the early nineteenth century, the Hausa kingship of Daura fell, as did most of Hausaland, to the conquering Fulanis of Usman dan Fodio's *jihad.* Daura's deposed king at the time, Sarkin Gwari Abdu, went into exile and died. Gwari's royal family, however, retained the hope of returning to Daura sometime in the future, and therefore reconstituted successive (although competing) governments in exile. One of these was established by Lukudi, Sarkin Gwari's son and designated successor, in Yardaji.

Yardaji served as Lukudi's capital-in-exile until about 1845, when it was attacked and taken by Ibram of Damagaram (also called Zinder). Ibram forced Lukudi to move to nearby Zango, where he would share his rulership with Lukudi's son Nuhu. (Naturally, this was under Damagaram's vassalage.) Zango remained the capital of the Daura Hausas in exile until 1906, when the British ousted the Fulanis from *birnin* (city) Daura, and restored the Sarkin Gwari Abdu's descendants and dynasty to power— albeit under British "protection"— in their ancestral capital.

The partition of Hausaland into the British and French colonies of Nigeria and Niger acutely affected the then existing boundaries of *kasar* (country) Daura. Not only were areas that had been subordinated to Zinder (including Zango) now wrested from Zinder control, but they now found themselves in a new country entirely— British Nigeria. (The reduced "sultanate" of Zinder found itself in French Niger.) The new emirate of British-controlled Daura was substantially larger than it had been under Fulani rule (although not as large as the Hausa kingdom of Daura prior to the Fulani takeover). The entire northern and most of the eastern edge of today's Daura emirate (a distance of approximately one hundred miles) still serves as frontier with the Republic of Niger; there is an official border-crossing station at Zango, and one can walk into Niger territory from the outskirts of Yardaji (less than one-half mile).

This proximity to Niger for the Daura emirate, and for Yardaji in particular, has been found to reinforce the consciousness of being part of Nigeria.[16] Far from yearning for reunification with Nigérien (albeit Hausa) people across the border, over half a century of colonial partition, and over a quarter of a century of independent Nigerian rule have created administrative, economic, and psychological realities rendering Yardaji (and of course Daura) uncontestably Nigerian in spirit and fact, as well as by territorial fiat. Even as border settlements (partially *because* of being border settlements), Daura and Yardaji have fully experienced the ramifications of belonging to (Northern) Nigeria. Geographical position has hardly resulted in insularity from political changes, processes, and events elsewhere in the region and country. (In terms of the 1983 elections, the most significant circumstance arising from Daura's border position was the allegation— never substantiated— that campaign workers were preparing to bring in Nigériens from across the border to vote for NPN.)

Daura, under the British, represented a classic instance of Indirect Rule. Traditional legitimacy was invoked through the return of the ruling Hausa dynasty; continuity was maintained under the marathon reign of Sarkin Abdurrahman, who even outlived British colonialism. (Abdurrahman died in 1966, having been emir of Daura for fifty-four years.) Gradual changes were made throughout Daura emirate, in terms of administrative readjustment and developmental progress. Zango, for instance, was made one of the five district areas in the emirate (the others were Maiadua, Sandamu, Baure, and Daura proper). Likewise, Yardaji was designated one of fifteen village areas within the Zango district. The system of NA was duly established, with Abdurrahman in charge (first as sole native authority and then, in 1954, chief-in-council). Technical and administrative departments were created in the fields of agriculture, forestry, education, public works, construction and maintenance of public wells, sanitation, health, veterinary services, police, prisons, treasury.

M. G. Smith has demonstrated in the case of Daura what Whitaker has argued for Northern Nigeria in general: namely, that changes wrought in the name of progress and westernization did not fundamentally reverse traditional norms and structures of powerholding. Heading virtually all of the above-mentioned departments, for instance, were sons of traditional rulers. Daura politics became more a case of dynastic rivalry than electoral or partisan conflict. "[N]either party politics, nor the conciliar pyramid, nor increases in taxation, local revenues, expenditure, prosperity, and literacy rates materially affected the traditional patterns of authority and deference that ordered the relations of Daura's rulers and people."[17]

In Daura as throughout the North, the principle of electoral politics was mitigated by the weight of history, custom, and culture: "ideas of popular accountability and representation were equally alien and inimical to this system of government . . . the populace was incapable of exploiting the new electoral institutions to improve its lot by reducing the power of its rulers."[18] Deference and loyalty to the traditional rulers (who also controlled the NA administration) translated into support for that political party best seen to uphold and buttress their legitimacy.

The dominance of NPC was hence at least as great in the town and villages of Daura as it was throughout Northern Nigeria in general. NEPU supporters were completely marginalized, and subject to imprisonment for such offenses as "abusing the emir and the Native Authority."[19] NPC candidates swept all offices in Daura emirate, from local executive councilorship to representative to the federal House of Assembly in Lagos. Perhaps the most ironic twist demonstrating the intimacy of modern (qua electoral and partisan) with traditional (qua dynastic and hered-

Photo courtesy of Kaduna State, Nigeria

Alhaji Muhammadu Bashar, the emir of Daura

itary) politics is that Daura's first First Republic representative to the Northern House of Assembly in Kaduna (naturally, as NPC candidate) is today the emir of Daura himself, Sarkin Daura Alhaji Muhammadu Bashar.

Despite the overwhelming success in Daura of NPC, as measured by their monopoly of elected offices, electoral politics as such does not seem to have enthused the populace at large. M. G. Smith records a "disturbingly small" degree of participation in local politics, which he attributes either to "popular indifference" or "public disinclination to participate in political party alignments."[21] K. W. Post also notes "[t]he comparative lack of interest in modern politics on the part of most people in the emirates."[22] Nevertheless, no matter what general apathy is said to have existed throughout the North, and Daura emirate in particular, the voters of Daura East and Daura West constituencies did participate in the 1959 elections at remarkable rates of 91.9 percent and 89.7 percent, respectively.[23] (This was slightly higher than the average for the North as a whole. It also takes into account the withholding of female suffrage in Northern Nigeria at the time.) (See Table 2.2.) It would appear that, even if the *sarakuna's* initial resistance to (or at least suspicion of) these democratic "intrusions" were felt by the *talakawa* as well, the former at least knew how to expediently mobilize the latter when there was no escaping the democratic game.

A NOTE ON THE "KANO CONNECTION"

Although Daura emirate had long since been detached from Kano province and apportioned to Katsina province, the historical and economic influence of the city of Kano hardly disappeared because of First Republic politics. Even today, as part of Kaduna state, the common folk of the emirate have greater contact and commonality with the ancient Hausa metropolis city of Kano than with the newer, and more ethnically heterogeneous, city of Kaduna, the administrative capital of the state. (Kaduna was founded by Lord Lugard early in this century as the headquarters for British administration of Northern Nigeria.)[24] While Katsina province and Kaduna state administration boundaries, voting constituencies, and electoral trends must perforce be invoked in analyzing Daura emirate politics, the political environment and culture of Kano cannot be disregarded.[25]

Table 2.2   Results of Northern Nigerian Elections
             (Daura Constituencies— 1959)

Constituency	NPC		NEPU		AG		Indpt.	
	Votes	%	Votes	%	Votes	%	Votes	%
Daura East (includes Yardaji)	10,970	68.1	2,690	16.7	2,459	15.3	--	--
Daura West	9,675	60.3	716	4.5	1,148	7.1	4,518	28.1

Source: K. W. Post, The Nigerian Federal Election of 1959, (London: Oxford University Press, 1963): Appendix D.

The politicking that has occurred during Kano province and state campaigns (including the influence of Mallam Aminu Kano and his NEPU and PRP parties), and outbursts or riots in Kano itself— such as the pro-emir attacks on the governor and the Maitatsine revolts of the 1980s— have hardly left the people of Daura indifferent. (Maitatsine is the common name given to Alhaji Mohammed Marwa who, as a self-proclaimed prophet, led a violent anti-establishment movement in Northern Nigeria. Maitatsine inveighed against western consumerism and technology, and advocated a quasi-heretical reinterpretation of Islamic belief and ritual.) The way the people of Daura viewed these events, perhaps more than what has been recorded as "Katsina province" or "Kaduna state politics," has shaped political attitudes in Daura state. (Many of the campaign songs presented in the Appendix, for example, were recorded during rallies in Kano state— and include many such references— but were subsequently distributed, sold, and listened to in Daura.) To a significant extent, way up in Daura, the more nebulous "Kano Connection" weighs more than the otherwise infamous "Kaduna Mafia."

YARDAJI RECOLLECTIONS

In Yardaji, the term used to refer to the time period discussed above is itself indicative of the villagers' perspective on Nigeria's original attempts to expand "democracy" throughout the country. Rather than using the Hausa equivalent of "First Republic," Yardaji-ites employ the more personalistic *"Lokacin Sardauna"*— the time of the sardauna of Sokoto and leader of the NPC, Sir Ahmadu Bello.

Two decades after his assassination in 1966, Ahmadu Bello's reputation in Northern Nigeria— if Yardaji may be used as a reference— bears out Whitaker's earlier prediction:

> [T]he *Sardauna* [will be established] in local legend as a powerful personification of those attitudes of cultural pride, inward-regarding self-sufficiency, and taste for command and hierarchy, which for better or worse may well remain ingrained indefinitely in the patterns of political leadership in the world of the emirates.[26]

Certainly, Ahmadu Bello does evoke powerful memories, and nostalgic reminiscences, in this part of Nigeria. (The image of the slain sardauna for the Hausa of Nigeria may in many respects be

likened to that of John F. Kennedy for Americans.)[27] Beyond
Bello's own reputation, however, references to "*Lokacin Sardauna*" reinforce the idea that the introduction of Nigerian
politics to Hausa villagers meant less an acceptance of democratization, egalitarianism, and universal suffrage than rallying
around traditional chiefs and leaders for local, regional, and ultimately national stakes in government.

Despite above-mentioned reports of general electoral apathy
in the North in general, and the Daura emirate in particular, there
were village advocates of both NPC and NEPU in Yardaji. Only
NPC, however, had much of a following. For one thing, according to one erstwhile Yardaji NPC supporter, both *sarakuna* and
masu-kudi— traditional chiefs and people of wealth—were very
much involved with the NPC. (The emir of Daura was himself said
to be the NPC leader in the emirate.) NPC members wore uniforms: "They would sew jackets and pants like policemen, and
people would be afraid to follow any other party." Indeed, there
was no *walwala* (happiness) if one joined another party; after
elections, members of opposition parties were known to be
beaten, and they would have their "new hair" (*suma*) forcibly cut
off. Of course, there was no place where they could then go to
complain, for all the authorities were themselves NPC.

All in all, the major difference between the First and Second
republics, according to Alhaji Usman of Yardaji, is that whereas
"during the time of the sardauna the NPC was much stronger
than all the others, now [i.e., during the Second Republic] there
are many parties with strength." To understand why this should
have been so, even in off-the-beaten-track Yardaji, we must consider those institutional, administrative, and constitutional
changes that had since taken place throughout all Nigeria.

STRUCTURAL CONSIDERATIONS

The assassinations and military coup of 1966 were the culmination of increasingly untenable ethnic and parliamentary strains
and contradictions in the First Republic. If it is indeed true that,
in Nigeria, "institutional architecture is a key to democratic viability,"[28] then Nigeria's first experience with post-independence
democracy can be likened to an elaborate and ornate tower that
toppled because the architects had neglected the pillars and
foundation.

In 1960, although none of its inhabitants probably ever viewed it in this way, Yardaji found itself integrated into a regional federation of a newly independent state governed by a quasi-British constitutional and parliamentary system. Yardaji, still part of the Daura emirate (and Katsina province), found itself in the largest and most heavily populated of the country's three (and then four) regions, the (Hausa-Fulani) North. (The others were the [largely Igbo] East and [largely Yoruba] West, out of which the Midwest region was carved in 1963.) As part of the North, Yardaji participated in elections that sent (mostly NPC) representatives to the 177-member regional Northern House of Assembly in Kaduna and to the 313-member federal House of Representatives in Lagos. (The NPC dominated in the federal government as well, with a 149-seat plurality in the House and a benighted NPC Hausa, Sir Abubakar Tafawa Balewa, as prime minister.) In addition, the North had an influential House of Chiefs (composed of seventy-six traditional rulers) that had the constitutional power to veto all legislation (except concerning the budget, which it could nevertheless delay for thirty days). Local government was controlled at the regional (as opposed to national) level, and partisan politics, as we have seen, was primarily a contest between the two Northern parties, NPC and NEPU.

After interethnic and interregional conflict toppled the civilian government in 1966, a succession of military regimes (Ironsi, Gowon, Murtala, Obasanjo) governed Nigeria for thirteen years. The constitution was disbanded, political parties were banned, and the armed forces ruled by edict. (Only in 1976 was a semblance of democracy restored at the local level.) During this time, Yardaji found itself reorganized into North-Central state (one of twelve states) in 1967, and then Kaduna state (one of nineteen states) in 1976. A Zango local government area (LGA) was created within the Daura emirate, which was itself administered by a military-appointed civilian administrator and council. State creation was seen as a critical administrative reform that would help shift allegiance from (and hence competition between) broad ethnic/regional groups and units to smaller, ethnically neutral state entities.

The Nigerian military had always promised a return to civilian rule (a term that is rather uncritically equated with "democracy"), but did not begin taking active steps to do so until the mid–1970s. A Constitutional Drafting Committee (CDC) was established in 1975, with a view toward drawing up a new constitutional framework under which parties, elections, and civilian government would be restored. Fundamental to the CDC's objectives was to restore electoral politics in a way that would diminish ethnic rivalry and heighten Nigerian unity *within* a system of partisan competitiveness. The result was a seemingly ingenious U.S.-style constitutional system that integrated Nigerian-specific safeguards against ethnic politics.[29]

Following the logic of administrative reform under the military, traditional Igbo vs. Yoruba vs. Hausa rivalries were supposed to wither away under a federal system of sundry states, replacing the in-built parliamentary pressure cooker which had fostered regional rivalry. In a like spirit, the CDC recommended a federal system of government with a directly elected president and vice-president (with single renewable four-year terms), a Senate with equal (five) representation from all states, a proportionally elected House of Representatives, popularly elected state governors, and state-level Houses of Assembly. Significantly, particularly for the states of the old North, the idea of reconstituting a House of Chiefs on the state level was rejected. Traditional rulers were accorded a formal place only in local government bodies, and were barred from actively participating in electoral or partisan politics. (Sitting chiefs could, of course, exercise their rights as citizens to vote in elections.) In the end, after considerable debate, the CDC also rejected the idea of a Shari'a (i.e., Islamic) federal Court of Appeals.

Provisions for the registration of political parties and requirements for election to office also marked a significant departure from First Republic ways. Nigeria's new constitution expressly forbade the establishment of ethnic, religious, or geographically exclusive parties; all parties, in other words, had to be *national* in scope and nature, and had to be open to all Nigerians, regardless of ethnicity, religion, homeland, or sex. Party headquarters had to be situated in the capital, and two-thirds of the country's nineteen states had to be represented on the executive committee of any party seeking legal recognition. Ministerial nominations had to include persons from every state in the country. Most important, a presidential candidate could be elected to office only if, in addition to receiving a majority or plurality of votes nationwide, he also received one-quarter of the votes in *two-thirds of the states throughout the federation.*[30]

It has been claimed that, because of these unique provisos, Nigeria's Second Republic constitution was more Nigerian than American, more African than western.[31] Viewed from the bush, however, this contention is implausible. People in Yardaji, like most of Nigeria's illiterate peasants, were worlds removed from that rather august body comprising the Constitutional Drafting Committee.[32] They had no understanding of the explicit terms of the constitution, and only a dim grasp of the need to operate their polity according to some written document. However consciously and diligently the intelligentsia of the CDC may have *tried* to indigenize Nigeria's new political framework and avoid a carbon-copy replica of the U.S. political system, what did finally emerge bore a much greater resemblance to the United States Constitution of 1787 than it did to anything with which the people of Daura emirate— ever since Bayajidda slew a snake, married their queen, and founded the Hausa Bakwai— had ever come into contact.

This is not to say that the constitution of Nigeria's Second Republic was ultimately irrelevant to the villagers of Yardaji. Although they may have had little if any concrete knowledge about it, to the extent that the constitution shaped and molded the parties that eventually did establish themselves in their emirate, local government area, and village, Yardaji-ites were eventually affected by decisions made by these otherwise remote constitutional framers. Indeed, the way in which "democracy" resurfaced in Yardaji, and the extent to which the village was politicized from without, was a reflection of many decisions made at the center, from a creation of more states to the requirement of broadly based, national backing for political parties. But in terms of relative distance from the original model, and from the vantage of the village, this latest constitution was no less an alien (qua U.S.) phenomenon than the First Republic's Westminsterlike parliament was a British one. After all, from a Hausa perspective, both were equally *Bature* (European).

CHAPTER THREE

The Parties: Nigeria

SECOND REPUBLIC PARTIES

This is not the place to provide an in-depth recapitulation of the parties and leaders of the Nigerian Second Republic in general, nor of the 1983 elections in particular. However, in order to discuss the role and perception of the parties in Yardaji in 1983, some discussion of what followed the 1978 lifting of the ban on politics, the formation of political parties on the national level, and the 1979 elections that inaugurated the Second Republic is in order.

When Lieutenant General Olusegun Obasanjo announced on September 21, 1978, "The ban on politics is lifted with effect from today and the state of emergency is also lifted,"[1] politicized Nigerians lost little time in reconstituting organized groups and parties to compete for national and state power. Fifty-two political associations initially sought recognition as political parties by the Federal Electoral Commission (FEDECO); thirty-five were granted application forms from FEDECO, and nineteen submitted them satisfactorily by the December 18 deadline.[2] Five were ultimately recognized by FEDECO as able to participate in the 1979 contest to reelect the first civilian government of the Second Republic.

The National Party of Nigeria (NPN) campaigned under the slogan, "One Nation, One Destiny, One God."[3] A single raised forefinger identified the NPN stalwart; the NPN emblem was a house flanked by maize plants. The platform of the NPN included

46

among its aims "one united strong Nigeria"; security for the individual, his property, and the nation as a whole (as protected by
the military and the police); national prosperity and self-reliance
(through a strong agricultural sector, rapid industrialization, and
equal opportunity); democratic rights, an open society, private
enterprise and initiative; and "adequate and sound education
based on high moral principles and African indigenous values."
NPN has been characterized as the most conservative of the Second Republic parties; its endorsement of the chieftaincy may be
cited as evidence: the party manifesto guarantees the recognition
of traditional rulers and institutions.[4]

The Nigerian People's Party (NPP) proclaimed, "Power to the
People." Its symbol was a four-member family (father, mother,
son, and daughter). Although it has been described as a "true
center party,"[5] NPP's official aim was to "fight relentlessly against
poverty, disease, ignorance, intolerance, indiscipline, feudalism,
racism, neo-colonialism and unjust exploitation of man by
man."[6] Its preferred means to build a self-reliant economy were:
achieving full employment of the nation's manpower and natural resources; mobilizing the rural masses for participatory
development; and incorporating the urban working class into the
management process.[7]

The national slogan of an offshoot of the NPP, the Great
Nigeria People's Party (GNPP), was, "Politics Without Bitterness."
Its emblem was a palm tree, rooster, and cow. GNPP strove for a
"virile and self-reliant economy"; industrialization with an "equi-
table distribution of fruits of economic development"; equal opportunity and higher living standards for all Nigerians (regardless
of age, religion, sex, or ethnic group); and national unity,
sovereignty, independence, and territorial integrity. The GNPP
also hoped to foster a "dynamic" foreign policy and a "secular
democratic state."[8]

"Four Cardinal Principles" marked the Unity Party of Nigeria
(UPN). These were: "free education at all levels NOW"; integrated
rural development (especially to boost food production); free
health care; and full employment. The UPN wanted to make
Nigeria "fulfill her destiny in the world to become a nation of great
economic opportunities . . .hardworking, economically com-
fortable, socially satisfied . . ." To do this, UPN needed to be in a
position to effectuate its "PLAN." The party's symbol was a
torchlight radiating nineteen rays over (a hitherto dark) Nigeria.[9]

The People's Redemption Party (PRP) was the one political
party which most explicitly advocated social revolution. "Wealth

and licentiousness for a few but deprivations and frustrations for the masses" was the way it described, and lambasted, Nigerian politics and society. Its "key" (the party's emblem) would unlock the door to social justice for the common man of Nigeria. PRP, a self-styled movement for progress, willingly challenged the forces of "privilege and conservatism." It characterized its own ideology as "Democratic Humanism."[10]

The ideals and platforms of these new Nigerian parties were lofty indeed. (Perhaps the "loftiest" party to emerge to contest the 1983 elections was the Nigerian Advance Party [NAP], with its "take the nation back to God programme.")[11] Yet, however high-minded party intellectuals and writers were, their otherwise populist platforms and manifestoes were only remotely accessible— logically, logistically, and linguistically— to the "common man." To complicate matters even further, it has been claimed that, ideologically, the parties were not all that different from each other, anyhow:

> [The] political parties were nothing more than unstable coalitions of ethnic notables who united together for the primary purpose of winning (rigging) elections and sharing offices.[12]
>
> The parties offer[ed] no real alternative choice to voters on the ideological scale. . . . By not offering meaningfully different choices in programmes and policies, the parties helped to reinforce the saliency of the personality, regional and ethnic factors in the elections.[13]

Such "personality, regional and ethnic factors" certainly continued to preoccupy the minds of many, if not most, observers and analysts of Nigerian politics. Ideologies aside, what mattered most was that these Second Republic parties seemed to be thinly veiled reincarnations of their First Republic forebears. The NPN, for instance, was widely regarded as the successor to the NPC: Alhaji Shehu Shagari, a native of Sokoto (and a Fulani-Hausa), emerged as the NPN presidential candidate and leader, bearing the mantle of the sardauna of Sokoto. With Mallam Aminu Kano leading it, the PRP suspiciously resembled NEPU. NPP was seen as a modern-day NCNC, especially since Dr. Nnamdi Azikiwe was the head of both. Ditto for UPN and the Action Group: Chief Obafemi Awolowo personified both versions of the "Yoruba party." And Alhaji Ibrahim Waziri's GNPP has also been identified with a less renowned First Republic political association, the Bornu

Youth Movement (BYM). (Waziri himself was a well-known politician from the earlier days, as a Northern minister with the NPC.)

Thus, the "new" parties were expected to find strength in their traditional bastions of support: the NPN and PRP in Northern (and particularly Hausa) states, the NPP in Eastern (and Igbo) states, the UPN in Western (and particularly Yoruba) states. GNPP was dismissed as a Borno state (i.e., Kanuri) phenomenon. The intervening constitutional, structural, and federalist changes would have served only to obfuscate otherwise clear and automatic ethnic and regionalist voting patterns. Thus, in a constituency such as Daura in Kaduna state, the only question was how well the PRP would fare against the NPN.

In fact, in the 1979 elections, the NPN emerged as the single most important party in Nigerian politics. Although it was with a much-contested plurality (Nigeria's supreme court had to rule whether he had actually received "one-quarter of the votes in two-thirds of the states"), the NPN's Shehu Shagari was elected as president of Nigeria with 5,688,857 votes, or 33.8 percent of the total number of officially recorded ballots cast. In Kaduna state, Shagari received 43 percent of the votes recorded as cast. In the Daura district (one of fourteen voting districts in Kaduna state), Shagari received 62 percent of the votes. (No figures are available for Yardaji's vote in 1979.) (See Table 3.1.)

In the gubernatorial elections, seven of the nineteen states went to NPN candidates. Critically, in Kaduna state the PRP candidate Balarabe Musa squeaked by his NPN opponent to become governor. (The difference was 9,353 votes, or only three-fourths of a single percentage point.) The Kaduna state Assembly, however, was solidly NPN (sixty-four out of ninty-nine seats). After many months of protracted stalemate between Kaduna's executive and legislative branches, the state Assembly eventually impeached the PRP Musa in 1981. (See Table 3.2.)

In terms of its federal representative in the Senate and House of Representatives, Kaduna state was also solidly NPN: ninteen out of thirty-three Kaduna representatives to the House were NPN, as were three out of five senators. (See Table 3.3.)

For Kaduna state in particular, as well as Nigeria as a whole, the inaugural elections of 1979 thus bestowed upon the NPN an electoral advantage that the party would exploit for the first four years of the Second Republic. Partisan dominance did not, however, translate into developmental efficiency. Although certain popular measures were taken (such as the lifting of cattle and head poll taxes in Kaduna and Kano states), no substantial

Table 3.1   Results of 1979 Presidential Elections

Candidate	Party	Daura District		Kaduna State		Nigeria Republic	
		Votes	%	Votes	%	Votes	%
Shagari	NPN	47,137	(62.3)	596,302	(43.1)	5,688,857	(33.8)
Kano	PRP	21,381	(28.2)	437,771	(32.3)	1,732,113	(10.3)
Waziri	GNPP	5,196	(06.8)	190,936	(13.8)	1,686,489	(10.0)
Awolowo	UPN	1,321	(01.7)	92,332	(06.6)	4,916,651	(29.2)
Azikiwe	NPP	521	(00.6)	65,371	(04.7)	2,822,523	(16.7)
Total		75,556		1,382,712		16,846,633	

Source: Nigerian Federal Electoral Commission (FEDECO).

Table 3.2   Kaduna State Results of 1979 Senate, House, and State Assembly Elections (by number of seats and percentage of votes cast)

	NPN	PRP	GNPP	UPN	NPP	Total
Senate	3 (37.8%)	2 (26.2%)	0 (22%)	0 (8%)	0 (5.8%)	5
House of Representatives	19 (39.6%)	10 (28.8%)	1 (20%)	1 (7%)	2 (4.4%)	33
State Assembly	64 (46%)	16 (21%)	10 (21%)	3 (6.4%)	6 (5.3%)	99

Source: Nigerian Federal Electoral Commission (FEDECO).

Table 3.3   All-Nigeria Results of 1979 Senate, House, and State Assembly Elections (by number and percentage of total seats)

	NPN	PRP	GNPP	UPN	NPP	Total
Senate	36 (37.9%)	7 (7.3%)	8 (8.4%)	28 (29.5%)	16 (16.9%)	95
House of Representatives	168 (37.4%)	49 (10.9%)	43 (9.6%)	111 (24.7%)	78 (17.4%)	449
State Assemblies	487 (36.1%)	144 (10.7%)	157(11.7%)	333 (24.7%)	226 (16.8%)	1,347

Source: Nigerian Federal Electoral Commission (FEDECO).

improvement in the material welfare of most Nigerians *outside* of (or unconnected to) government was to be seen. To the contrary, economic mismanagement, austerity, and "squandermania" were seen to afflict the country at large. Certainly, the severe drop in oil revenues to the federal government (as a result of plummeting international prices) did nothing to help Nigeria's economic situation; but neither could such externalities fully explain why clinics were bereft of the medicines they were supposed to provide, or why schoolteachers were going months without being paid. While few expressed regard and nostalgia (at least openly) for the passing of military rule, civilian government was falling short of the expectations that the 1979 return to democracy had promised. Nevertheless, when the constitutionally mandated period for new elections arrived, election fever reinfected the country.

CAMPAIGN, 1983

On the eve of the 1983 elections, there were six legally registered parties vying for power throughout Nigeria. In addition to the five parties that had competed in 1979 (NPN, UPN, GNPP, NPP, and PRP), the Nigeria Advance Party (NAP), led by presidential aspirant Tunji Braithwaite, was recognized as a valid political party by FEDECO.

NAP never attained the significance of the other "big five," and was especially marginal in the Northern states. Braithwaite and the NAP proclaimed "nine sign-posts of changes," a revolutionary program that alone could cure Nigeria of its "perennial paralysis and decadence."[14] Some of the more noteworthy "sign-posts" were: YOU (Youniversal Electrification System); FLOW (Full Level Of Water); READ (Revolution, Education, Action for Development); HIP (Health Insurance Policy); SOCIALISM (qua "freedom from harassment by bigmanism"); and the eradication of mosquitoes and rats from Nigeria.[15]

Under the incumbent president Alhaji Shehu Shagari, the National Party of Nigeria was considered a shoo-in for a second term. That NPN, with its conservative (by Nigerian standards) and status-quo orientation would again be Northern in complexion— and again be supported by the Hausa-Fulani "aristocracy"— was a given. The greater question was the extent to which four years of Shagari incumbency and NPN national rule would translate into an even larger, more widespread constituency throughout the entire country.

NPN's sibling rival was still the People's Redemption Party. Even more than the NPN, the PRP was primordially associated with the Hausa North; PRP, however, carried its familiar banner of radical, and populist, change. Mallam Aminu Kano led the party, as presidential candidate, for much of the campaign. In April of 1983, however—just four months before the elections were to be held—Aminu Kano died. With him went much of the momentum and popularity with which he personally had invigorated NEPU in the First, and personified PRP in the Second, Republic.

The Nigerian People's Party, headed by the veteran politician "Zik" (Dr. Nnamdi Azikiwe), tried to expand its traditional base of support beyond the Eastern states and the Igbo people. One successful bid was to recruit the erstwhile PRP governor of Kano state, Alhaji Abubakar Rimi, into the NPP.

Chief Obafemi Awolowo continued to lead the Unity Party of Nigeria. Observers characterized the UPN in 1983 as still essentially Yoruba in composition and backing. Even in the far North, though, the UPN leader was familiarly known and referred to by his nickname, "Awo."

Four years after the beginning of the Second Republic, Ibrahim Waziri's Great Nigeria People's Party seemingly lost more ground than any other party. Having carved out a modest niche in the northeast in 1979, GNPP was not vulnerable to NPN's nationwide growth, which naturally included the recapturing of regionally renegade GNPP territory. GNPP's ideological differentiation from NPP also made its second-term bid all the more problematic.

Despite the non-ethnic and non-regionalist thrust to the Second Republic constitution (to be elected president, as we have seen, a candidate had to receive at least one-quarter of the vote in at least two-thirds of the states), political analysis of the 1983 elections was largely reduced to the familiar formulae of "ethnic arithmetic." UPN was not expected to carry much more than the Yoruba vote; likewise, for NPP with the Igbos. PRP was a factor in only two Northern states (Kano and Kaduna), and GNPP in one (Borno). The big question mark was the extent to which the NPN, given its four years of incumbency, had managed to make inroads into non-Northern, non-Hausa states, and truly transcend "ethnic politics." Massive electoral fraud, and the ensuing military coup, perhaps preclude ultimate judgment on these questions. For our purposes here, however, it is the party-ethnicity identity that we wish to examine.

No constituency could be regarded as more Northern, or more Hausa, than Daura emirate in general, and the village of Yardaji in particular. Not a single southerner resided in Yardaji, and only scattered Igbo traders populated the emirate. No one in Yardaji knew more than a word or two of Igbo or Yoruba, and only a handful (the schoolteachers and secondary school students home on vacation) could communicate in English. If the politics of ethnicity were as supreme as often contended, then Yardaji would have been exclusively NPN and/or PRP territory. In fact, not only were the "non-Hausa parties" represented in the village and the emirate, but their themes and platforms were "Hausafied" to generate local popularity and acceptance.

CHAPTER FOUR

The Parties: Yardaji

UPN — LIGHT IN THE BUSH

U P N

Haske ("light") was the (Hausa) motto for (Yoruba) Awolowo's Unity Party of Nigeria. Usman dan Illela was the village leader of UPN in Yardaji; he was appointed to this position by Alhaji Modaha, the UPN leader in Zango.

According to Illela, prior to 1983 only NPN and PRP were represented in Yardaji. But when Modaha came to the village and said that UPN would bring the people of Yardaji "into light, and out of darkness," people rallied round. (Modaha also promised one car, six motorcycles, and ten bicycles for UPN campaigns.) Illela claimed six hundred UPN "supporters" (*goyon baya*— literally "carrying on back," as mothers do with infants) in Yardaji alone. UPN, said Illela, would "rescue" and "save" the *talakawa* (common people), by giving work to the unemployed and bringing down prices.

As with all the opposition parties, UPN (and Illela) accused the incumbent NPN of inflation, dishonesty, corruption, and economic mismanagement. He spoke sitting beneath a neam tree, to which a UPN poster was affixed.

We Welcome You AWO to Kaduna State

The Leader
The Scholar
The Economist
The Political Genius
The Teacher
The World-Class Author
The Mentor
The Philosopher
The Cleanser

The fact that the poster was in English and hence incomprehensible to Illela (as well as to 99 percent of the village) was irrelevant; the sheer presence of the signs and symbols of "modern" politics can be as significant as the message that the symbols are trying to convey.

The main symbol of the UPN campaign, at least to villagers throughout Daura emirate, was the blue Volkswagen beetle. Motor vehicles were a crucial index of party strength, both in terms of status attributed by villagers to the parties as well as the favors that parties, by offering lifts, could do for villagers. All the other parties (except for NAP) had minibuses at their disposal; whether UPN's pool of blue beetles was a deliberate attempt to be distinctive, or whether it represented the party's financial austerity (at least in the North), is unknown. But even the youngest children in the village soon came to recognize the UPN beetle, collectively yelling "Awo, Awo!" (the local diminutive of "Awolowo") whenever the blue VW made its periodic appearance.

Alhaji Modaha, when interviewed in Zango, elaborated on Mallam Illela's reasons for supporting UPN. (He too, as with most party activists in Zango and Yardaji, is a farmer.) Everyone was tired of the Shagari government, claimed Modaha, tired of the inflation, tired of the high prices. UPN cared for all parts of the country, including the bush. Awolowo, he went on, was disinterested in the salary attached to the office.

When the interviewer pointed out that Awolowo is not Hausa, Alhaji Modaha was emphatic with his rejoinder. "He is a son of Nigeria!" he insisted. "Because there is a mixture of tribes in Nigeria, we need a mix in government— Hausas, Christians, all kinds." Then, by way of example, he rhetorically asked if the questioner were Hausa. When the obvious negative response was elicited, he continued: "Just because you're not Hausa, does that stop me from agreeing with you?" ("No.") "You go along with whom you're at peace, and feel good about—with the one who puts your mind to rest." Alhaji Modaha concluded by saying he was elected local UPN leader by the people in and around Zango, and that he wished to become Zango's representative in the Kaduna state House of Assembly.

NPP — "CHANGE"

No other party so dramatically demonstrated the success of transethnic politics in rural Hausaland as did the Nigerian People's Party. NPP's nominal leader, and 1983 presidential candidate, was the veteran Igbo politician, Dr. Nnamdi Azikiwe (better known as "Zik"); to the people of Yardaji, however, NPP was associated foremost with Alhaji Sani, a native son of the village who became a member of the Kaduna state housing authority and the Zango district NPP candidate for the state House of Assembly.

NPP's motto, at least throughout Hausaland, was *canji* ("change"). Alhaji Sani recounted the familiar litany of things which needed to be changed— especially an incumbent president who was ruining the country and driving up prices— and he described the kinds of changes NPP would bring: e.g., electricity and running water to the village, medicine to Yardaji's dispensary. With great enthusiasm and imagery, he also promised that his party would bring two-lane highways to Kaduna state.

Alhaji Sani expressed resentment that the incumbent NPN state assemblyman never visited Yardaji. His own leader was Azikiwe, Alhaji Sani declared, even though "Zik" was neither Hausa nor Muslim.

Although Alhaji Sani was the Yardaji NPP advocate with the greatest notoriety, the official NPP leader in the village was Alhaji Amadou. Alhaji Amadou expressed the defiance toward traditional leadership for which the party of *canji* was so well known. "We don't want traditional rulers [the emirs, the district heads, the village heads] to stick their noses [*sau baki*, literally, "to put their mouths"] into politics. It's all right that they be greeted, officiate at marriages and all that—but beyond that, they should go their way, and we (the *talakawa*) ours. NPN wants to use the traditional rulers to restore the poll tax and cattle tax. NPP will fight to prevent this."

Mallam Salissou, a petrol seller and NPP leader in Zango, elaborated on the tyranny (*zalunci*) of the NPN government: "There is so much wealth in the country, but not among the *talakawa*. NPN takes money for itself, and sends the nation's resources (*dukiya kasa*) out of the country. . . .We want traditional leaders to remain, but only so they act in accordance with Allah's laws." Mallam Salissou swore— "upon the Book"— that if elected, NPP would accomplish its work (bring in running water, electricity) within three months. He also invoked Azikiwe's recent campaign pledge, which appealed immensely to Nigeria's Sahelian citizens in the Northern hinterlands: "Zik" would plant trees all along the border with Niger Republic, to stop the Sahara from entering Nigeria.

GNPP — "JUSTICE!"

G N P P

Mohammad Usman Naauwa, a driver by profession, was head of the Zango branch of the GNPP, as well as candidate for the state House of Assembly. His advocacy for the GNPP platform (*manufofi*) was spirited.

A GNPP victory, claimed Usman, would bring *adalci* ("justice," the party's motto) to common folk. Taxes would remain abolished; the economy (*tattalin arziki*) would nevertheless be buoyed. Usman insisted on the peaceableness of his party, in contrast to the others, for whom "politics" meant "animosity." GNPP stood for *soyayya da zaman lafiya*: love, health, and prosperity. GNPP wanted only peace with the other parties, while victory for these others would lead only to fighting. Once GNPP was in power, it would consult the communities and provide what they wanted, be it running water, a paved road, or a functioning hospital.

On a personal note, Usman Naauwa volunteered why he had joined GNPP rather than any other party: "Because I am a nationalist [*kishin kasa*]." He believed in civic service (*bautawa kasa*), both for his native Zango and for the country as a whole.

In Yardaji itself, GNPP's liaison was the sardonic tailor Alhaji Salissou, who kept an unusually tight mouth about his political views and activities, preferring instead to hear about the researcher's. Perhaps this is what enabled him his partisan flexibility, abandoning not only his party's village leadership but the GNPP entirely, just weeks prior to the actual election. Alhaji Salissou, invoking a series of unkept GNPP promises, then became an active supporter of *canji* (NPP).

PRP — RADICALS IN ROBES

P R P

Unlike UPN, NPP, and even GNPP, PRP was universally recognized to be a purely "Hausa party," thus finding fertile ground in Daura-Zango-Yardaji territory. In line with the opposition parties, however, PRP was also a populist party, presenting itself as the defender of the oppressed, common people (*talakawa*) against the entrenched, vested interests of the ruling class (*sarakuna*).

The death of Mallam Aminu Kano (affectionately known as *Babba*, or "Daddy") just four months prior to the 1983 elections upset the PRP's campaign momentum, even in the Northern states. (It also gave rise to some petty barbs by the party's competitors, who began referring to the PRP as the *masu-maraya*, the "orphans' party.") But PRP's message was continued by such party faithfuls as Shafiu Halilu, Zango's PRP leader and state House candidate; Abdul Hamidou, the party's leader in Yardaji; and Mallam Sule, Yardaji's PRP "secretary."

Shafiu Halilu explained the symbolism of the PRP flag. Red stood for the difficulty, the suffering that the *talakawa* undergo. White represented the happiness (*farin ciki*, or "white heart") that all would feel if PRP were to win. And black symbolized *bakin fata 'yan Afirka*— the black men of Africa, all of whom should achieve freedom and independence. The party's symbol was the key, "to release kindness for the common man" [*bude talaka, bude alheri*] while "locking away pain and dishonesty" [*kulle cuta, kulle hainci*]. PRP's motto was Nasara, "Victory."

Shafiu, without knowing it, used Hausa language to advocate Marxist ideology. "There should be no rich, and no poor [*Ba mai-kudi, ba talaka*). . . . According to the PRP constitution, everyone should be given work. Every person is entitled to his own freedom and independence [*'yanci*]. . . . A common man can go to the government, and tell it what he needs, and what he desires. There will be no more dependence on the rich— only upon the government, which will help him." In short, "the PRP wants the common man to be enlightened [*kansa ya waiye*)." Shafiu then elaborated on the role of the rich, and poor, in the other parties:

Mallam Salissou (under the poster), NPP organizer

Shafiu Halilu (standing, right) with other PRP stalwarts

In all the other parties, you can find rich men. . . . They will give
people money to campaign for them, but then these people are
"bought." They won't have their 'yanci afterwards to go say, "Bring
us electricity, bring us water"—because they've already been paid.
Even I, a common man—my father is a mere farmer—I'll be able to
go right to the government, and talk to it. . . . If I were in NPN—because I am a common man, because my father has no money, and
is not royalty—I would never get to this position (as candidate for
state House of Assembly, chairman of Zango branch PRP). . . . Our
party [unlike the others] doesn't have money. For the campaign, we
do it ourselves—our party doesn't give us money.

Shafiu was one of the few persons to discuss Nigeria as a
whole, and the Biafran War in particular: "PRP wants to stop
tribalism [daina kabilanci]. [But]. . . . Igbos and Yorubas want
to cut off the North from the rest of the country. If they are elected,
they will show tribalism, as they did in the past. . . . There is oil,
petrol in the South. There was a war over it. But Allah had the
North win—to keep the country as one." He also expressed the
strongest feelings against the other rival parties:

> NPP is an Igbo party. . . . It is strong in the south. . . . It will
> show tribalism.
> GNPP makes promises it won't be able to keep. In 1979, Waziri
> Ibrahim said he would give everyone money—but he didn't. . . .
> UPN is a tribalist party. If elected, they will cause violence
> [tashin hankali]. For example, it wants to bring the capital back to
> Lagos from Abuja, from the North. . . .[1] UPN wants to bring Israel
> to Nigeria. . . . It also wants Muslims to become Christians, and to
> leave Islam. . . .

In Yardaji itself, Abdul Hamidou and Mallam Sule brought
the PRP ideology back down to a villager's consciousness: "PRP
feels pity for the people," stated Abdul Hamidou. "It did away with
the poll tax, the cattle tax, and the inheritance tax. It loves the
common man—it builds roads, it brings water. It tends to the
health and well-being of the community [yana kiwon lafiya
jama'a.]"
Mallam Sule most eloquently expressed PRP's "liberation ideology":

> PRP seeks Mr. Everyman's freedom from servitude ['yanci dan
> Adam a kan bauta). There is too much ignorance and illiteracy

[*jahilci*], especially in the North. We must drive it away. . . . We must increase knowledge [*ilmi*], both in town and countryside. We are for free primary school education. . . .

Farming, herding, trading— this is what PRP is most concerned about. And every trade should be helped. . . . PRP is supported by farmers, traders, herders, blacksmiths, builders, and weavers. But those who accumulate lots of money— they are not for PRP. . . .

We do not tolerate the oppression [*zalumci*] of bygone years— that traditional leaders be on top. In the past, they would tax before anything else— people would have to sell their millet to pay the taxes. The common people were obliged to bring gifts to the emir, and to carry them on their heads [for great distances], by foot. . . . Traditional leaders still butt into politics, but secretly. They should retain their royal titles [*sarauta*] and salaries [but . . . .] our leaders should be elected. . . . [Our goal is] that every person, of every tribe, be listened to— that all breathe equally. . . .

NPN — PEACE WITH POWER

N P N

The moderate (or conservative), status quo orientation of the incumbent NPN was indicated by the party's two bywords: friendship (*aminci*) and peace (*zaman lafiya*). Continued NPN rule, it was argued, would preclude the hotheadedness, instability, and violence (*tashin hankali*) that the other, less responsible parties threatened. NPN was consequently most strongly identified with the traditional leaders of the pre-colonial Hausa-Fulani establishment; incumbent President Alhaji Shehu Shagari himself hailed from Hausa-Fulani descent in Sokoto, the nineteenth century capital of the Fulani empire.

On the village level, NPN philosophy was the most consistent with those traditional norms of deference, respect, and loyalty that pervade the Hausa polity or hierarchy. Alhaji Usman, Yardaji head of the NPN, put it most succinctly: "The royal, the learned, and the wealthy— these are the important people on earth [*maisarauta, mallamai, mai-kudi, sune manya a duniya*]. These are the people who also make up the NPN. So we should go to their side, and show them our support." Hapshe, a Yardaji woman, summed up the attitude of many a villager: "NPN is the best party because it is the party of the chiefs and emirs [*sarakuna*], and of tradition [*gargajiya*). The other parties make noise, and pester

people [with their minibuses and bullhorns]. It is better to stay
with the one that does things quietly."

Alhaji Awali Cha'aibu Nakande Zango had a name as impressive as his position: NPN head in the Zango area. (He is also a
prominent Zango trader.) Alhaji Awali stressed the nationwide
appeal of NPN, as opposed to the ethnic and regional bases of the
other parties.

GNPP was the first party to appear in Zango, he explained,
but it didn't get along with the traditional leaders. PRP was only
a one-man party (that of Aminu Kano), and had backing only in
the North. UPN too was identified with a single man, and belonged
to the Yorubas; it tried by "buy the Hausa" with money. NPP is
an Igbo party, he went on, and also gives money to "buy" non-
Igbo support. NPN, however, has united the Hausa, Igbo, and
Yoruba. It has put together workers, traders, and farmers. It is
supported in the "hearts of the people." He claimed that NPN, unlike the other parties, didn't give away money, payments, or food
in its campaign. Shehu Shagari, Alhaji Awali concluded, was the
only candidate of peace, and cared for all of Nigeria; the others
cared only about their tribe or their state.

The above discussion of party leaders and their viewpoints in
the village of Yardaji and the nearby town of Zango should illuminate two major, and perhaps unexpected, phenomena: the poli-
ticization of the peasantry, and the transethnic composition of
the parties. Even such an ethnically, religiously, and linguistically homogeneous peasant community as Yardaji openly sub-
scribed to diverse and competing political parties. Perhaps not
all of the villagers' support was philosophically or ideologically
motivated, as the frequent allegations of parties "buying" potential voters attest; yet, even so, it is highly significant that the
often-touted supremacy of "tribalism" in African politics should
be vulnerable to as innocuous a thing as "dash" (as Nigerian colloquialism would put it). Nevertheless, that all village support for
"non-Hausa" parties stemmed from selfish or hypocritical mo-
tives remains to be substantiated.

Moreover, the readiness of many Hausa peasants to vocalize
their opposition to the leader of their country— one who was
nevertheless, like them, a Muslim Hausa— is remarkable. Many
a Yardaji-ite declared that it was the man that counted, not his
religion, language, or origin. And even if the majority of the village did ultimately vote for Shagari, reasons of principle (e.g., respect for tradition, maintenance of the chieftaincies) competed

with those of ethnic or religious identification. As one Yardaji UPN follower put it: *Siyasa, ba addini ba ne—* "politics isn't religion." To assert that Yardaji support for NPN was a simple matter of "ethnopolitics" is to oversimplify, and distort, a more nuanced reality.

CHAPTER FIVE

The Skeptics

Despite the evidence of partisan mobilization of the peasants in Yardaji in the 1983 campaign— as borne out by the above interviews with local party leaders— it would be misleading to convey the impression that the villagers unequivocally participated in, or even welcomed, the electoral campaign. In fact, concomitant with the animated level of campaigning by activist villagers was a more pervasive distrust, if not cynicism, for civilian "democratic" government. Significantly, disillusionment with, and cynicism for, electoral politics was expressed by many of the party activists themselves. Political activism stemmed more from a pragmatic accommodation to a system that the villagers could not control than from any belief in electoral democracy as such. Most Yardaji-ites, in fact, ruefully recalled the days of military rule (*mulkin soja* 8), when justice was perhaps meted out severely but at least in a relatively honest way.

Yardaji's unified hostility to, and rejection of, politics and politicians was made public early in the campaign, months prior to the actual elections. In a unique display of village policy to the outside world, the *samariya* (youth group) of Yardaji posted a signboard at the junction of the road leading to the village, with a message (in Hausa) for would-be stumpers:

Warning: We Don't Want It.

The People of Yardaji Have No Regard For Any Political Party Whatsoever. We Are Tired of Hearing Idle Talk. Whoever Ignores This Advice Will Regret It. Listen Well: Don't Come Here. This Is Not a Matter of One Person Alone. We Don't Want It. This Concerns Everyone. Forewarned is Forearmed.[1]

The recurrent theme of the message— "We Don't Want It" (*Ba Mu So*)— became a veritable battle cry of the village. Whenever a campaign bus would roll into Yardaji (nobody took the threats implied in the sign seriously), hordes of youngsters would spontaneously besiege the encroacher with jeers of "*Ba mu so!*" inviting the vehicle to leave.

The decision to discourage— if not threaten— candidates from campaigning in the village stemmed from a collective disgust with the manifold broken promises made during the previous (1979) elections. At that time, party representatives reputedly promised the villagers that, in return for their support, they would provide those amenities that Yardaji sorely lacked, e.g., *ruwan pompo* (mechanical water taps), *wuta* (electricity), and *hanya na gargadi* (a paved road connecting Yardaji with Zango). Four years later, with none of these promises fulfilled, many villagers reacted by rejecting the political parties *en masse*. Interestingly, it was not the particular party that had been in power that was blamed; *all* the parties were held responsible for the government's neglect of the village (or politics' failure to deliver). Indeed, numerous conversations revealed that there was no connection in the villagers' minds between the perceived obligation that a party should keep its electoral promises and the successful election of that party to power. That is, previously defeated parties were criticized, just as much as victorious ones, for not fulfilling their campaign promises.

Part of the reason would seem to lie in the expectations that parties generated throughout the campaign, and the largesse that they proved capable of displaying, at least to individuals. One Yardaji lad returned from a UPN rally in Kaduna, the state capitol, claiming that "Awo" had given away a million naira. He too was to be given money, he said— from the UPN secretary in Zango. UPN also promised two bicycles and one motorcycle to its Zango representative. It was acknowledged that UPN Volkswagens, ostensibly for campaign use, were kept and treated as personal property.

A former GNPP supporter abandoned his party because it "didn't give anything." He subsequently joined the NPN, which gave him three hundred naira, for distribution throughout the village in one-, two-, and three-naira amounts. (This villager reputedly gave away only fifty of the naira, "eating the greater portion" himself. He did, however, go out campaigning for the party.)

NPP had a respectable image amongst the people, because it gave away extremely large sums of cash. One man in Yardaji was said to have made a pilgrimage to Mecca with money NPP had given him. PRP also used to give away money, but this stopped after the death of the party's leader; Aminu Kano himself was said to have been a big giver of money, distributing twenty and thirty naira to ordinary people.

As the date of the elections approached, Yardaji's self-declared withdrawal from the political process gradually dissipated. The excitement and bustle of the campaign in nearby towns (particularly Zango and Daura) was too great to ignore. Whether Yardaji participated or not, Nigeria was proceeding with the elections; the policy of absolute rejection gave way to one of resigned, or partial, accommodation. The village *samariya* met once again, and, two months before the actual elections, decided to conditionally allow official politicking by outsiders. It was suggested that, as a condition to campaign, prospective officeholders be obliged to give a written pledge to keep their promises to the village. This policy was never put into effect, any more than the warning on the junction signboard was. It did, however, demonstrate the continued suspicion with which the villagers viewed the entire process, even as they yielded to the inevitable, and accepted the reality of the 1983 campaign. Campaign vehicles were now subjected to a cacophony of spirited chants, combining the traditional jeer of rejection (*Ba mu so*— "We don't want it!") with party slogans for support (*Canji-Dolle! Pawa!*— "Change is Necessary!" "Power!").

Throughout the campaign, villagers openly expressed their antipathy to politicians and politics. In contrast to the days of military rule, now "money corrupts truth" (*kudi cinye gaskiya*). An even more common refrain was *siyasa, ta bata duniya* ("politics has spoiled the world"). Neither were villagers reluctant to make specific accusations: "The Governor [of Kaduna state] is a thief. He is no different from someone who steals from your house. He takes the money of the public, and brings it to his own home."

Likewise, villagers roundly denounced the governor of Kano state for the disrespect he showed the emir of Kano in an incident in which the PRP governor accused the emir of several violations of the latter's administrative prerogatives. (The incident touched off antigovernment riots in the city of Kano, resulting in the burning of government buildings and the death of eleven persons, including the governor's political advisor.)[2]

It is to be emphasized that these Yardaji-ite expressions of dissatisfaction with civilian rule and electoral politics— stemming from broken campaign promises, official corruption, and perceived disrespect for traditional rulers— long preceded the coup that was to put an end to the Second Republic. (Diamond substantiates this on a more aggregate level, with his survey of 880 persons in both Kano city and outlying districts.)[3] It is *not* the case that popular criticism of civilian politics was promoted only *after* the coup, to legitimize the military's action. Even in the bush, electoral activities had long been tainted in villagers' eyes. When the campaign was brought to their own village, wizened Yardaji-ites reacted with at best some amount of cynicism, at worst a tinge of disgust. Few would not, when pressed, admit to at least a certain degree of skepticism.

CHAPTER SIX

Electoral Politics in Hausa Garb

There is nothing exceptional about the suspicion of politics as a process, and the disgust for politicians as a class, by Hausa peasants in Nigeria. Even in societies where electoral politics constitutes a universally accepted, institutionalized form of government, citizens often make comments similar to the ones expressed in Yardaji, concerning the dishonesty and hypocrisy of the political game and its actors. To understand, however, the extent to which modern, electoral politics represented a systemic threat to community life in Yardaji— and thereby sowed the seeds of its own discrediting— we need to delve deeper into the culture and values of Hausa life in general. Such a perspective should bear out the contention that village repudiation of politics stemmed not from any deficiencies or breakdown in Nigeria's peculiar system of democracy, but from a more fundamental contradiction between the norms and values inherent in Hausa society, and those implicit in western-style, electoral democracy.

The structural description of indigenous Hausa government (its hierarchy of *sarki, hakimi, mai-gunduma, mai-gari,* and *mai-unguwa,* or emir, district head, village area head, village chief, and ward head) has been described above. It remains now to describe the substance of Hausa political culture, particularly at the local, or village, level. To do this, two separate but complementary approaches will be taken. The first will highlight the values and standards of conduct that Hausa culture aims to impart to all members of its society. The second will focus on the norms and values that take on specifically political overtones. It will then be argued that, in terms of both the behavior that politicians in a multiparty system unavoidably assume, as well as the core values bound up with electoral democracy, modern politics engenders personal conduct and ideological principles that are not only alien to rural Hausa culture and society but positively at variance with it.

THE VIRTUOUS MAN

Kirk-Greene discusses the ensemble of qualities or attributes that define the virtuous man (*mutumin kirki*) in Hausa culture. Together, these qualities (Kirk-Greene identifies ten of them) imbue a man not only with inner worth but also with popular respect (*farinjini*– also translated as "popularity"). Since politicians by definition require popularity to survive, it is important that they command *farin jini* in the eyes of the people. Five qualities of virtue are particularly relevant here.

Truth and trust (*gaskiya* and *amana*) are the two pillars of the virtuous man in Hausa society. *Gaskiya* connotes more than honesty; it means reliability as well. A liar (*mai-karya*), of course, is despised as much as the man of *gaskiya* is esteemed. As for trust's antipode: "the sin of *cin amana*, to embezzle or convert something entrusted to one's care . . . ranks as an exceedingly grave blemish of character among the Hausa."[1] *Karamci* (generosity) far surpasses its equivalent concept in Anglo-Saxon culture. To be generous in Hausa society means more than giving away one's surplus to others; it entails the rather extravagant (to western eyes) display– and distribution– of wealth to the community. Stature and respect adheres to the big-spender; Hausa society has nothing akin to western social disapproval of ostentatious or flashy displays of wealth (indeed, such displays thrive) as long as the wealth is not only advertised but spread around.

An appreciation of *karamci* is necessary before one uncritically condemns, as many observers have, "bribery" and "corruption" in Nigerian politics. So is an understanding of the Hausa concept of money, and its noncommercial transfer from patron to client. As Polly Hill (1972) points out, in Hausaland money does not have the stigma of "filthy lucre" as it often does in the west.[2] Bank notes are ordinarily passed from one person to another in appreciation for little favors, as expressions of joy or affection, and out of mere happiness or friendship. In the case of social unequals, monetary gifts serve as confirmation of the patron's obligation and duty to his client, as well as the client's recognition of his patron's stature and superiority. A person who has money— as any politician is assumed to— and does *not* give it away is committing the social transgression of *rowa* (miserliness). As manifested in *barantaka* (clientship), to hand someone, especially a social inferior, a cash gift in public is neither improper, unseemly, nor demeaning; to withhold such a gift when appropriate, in contrast, may be an affront to a person's *mutunci* (self-respect). And, as Kirk-Greene points out, "the vice of *cin mutunci*, to humiliate a person by depriving him of his self-respect . . . is one of the worst sins in the roll-call of reprehension in Hausa society."[3]

This is not to argue that the fantastic sums of money given away by parties and politicians to influence the course of the 1983 Nigerian elections may be completely whitewashed by invoking traditional African concepts of generosity and gift-giving. Villagers more than anybody recognize that there are bounds beyond which *karamci* may constitute *cin hanci* (bribery). But those bounds are not always clearly defined (especially to westerners), and the relative propriety of money transfers to curry goodwill and favor (in the absence of out-and-out extortion) may be a fuzzy area to the Hausas themselves. When outside observers categorically condemn overt and systematic campaign payments to individuals as "political corruption" (especially when they carry their own psychocultural baggage about money as a stigmatized social lubricator), they obscure a more fundamental issue: the appropriateness of an ideologically based party system of government in a fundamentally materioclientalistic polity and culture.

Hakuri— patience— is often associated with the notion of *rabo*, or submission to the will of Allah. Often thought of (misleadingly) as "fatalism," *rabo* asserts that ultimately nothing happens without God's acquiescence or approval. This includes electoral results just as much as it does matters of life and death. Hence, the frustration of any would-be pollster in traditional Hausa society, wishing to glean voters' electoral preferences:

Q: Whom do you support in the upcoming elections?
A₁: Whomever Allah chooses, he is the one that I prefer.
A₂: The one that Allah brings, he'll be elected.
                              or
Q: Why do you prefer the____party?
A: Because that's the one that my heart is drawn to.

Beyond truth, trust, generosity, and patience (or submission), Kirk-Greene mentions a fifth criterion of the "virtuous man" that will inform a Hausa's evaluation of any prospective leader: good manners, or *ladabi* : "*Ladabi* is the courteous behavior obligatory towards all those who traditionally earn such respect: those in positions of authority like *mallam* the teacher, *alkali* the judge, *sarki* the chief . . . [L]adabi can be interpreted as the outward manifestation of that ready obedience which permeate[s] the Hausa attitude to legitimate authority."[4]

Ladabi is thus related to *biyayya* (obedience, loyalty) to one's elders or hierarchical superiors. Its antithesis is represented by *zage-zage*, abusive, insulting, and belittling language. *Zage* is the "commonest vehicle" of *cin mutunci*, which, we have seen, "is one of the worst sins in the roll-call of reprehension in Hausa society."

Even if absolute obedience to one's social superiors is impossible—especially in the context of modern political life—Hausa culture demands that disagreement be manifested with the appropriate degree of respect or propriety. And this is where the rough and tumble of electoral politics butts so strongly against the (Hausa) cultural norm of protocol. It is also what alienated the villagers of Yardaji from their country's chosen (if imported) method of electoral politics.

According to Hausa peasants, politicians, by definition, are dishonest. "They make promises [*alkawari*] so that people will support them, but, once elected, they do not keep their word [*basu cika magana*]." Most indictingly, the politicians themselves can be quite forthright about their own hypocrisy (*manafunci*). "I have to go and tell lies now," a candidate for the state House of Assembly announced quite candidly, as he prepared to attend a rally. "That's what 'campaigning'[5] is all about—tell the people what you'll bring and give them if elected, even when you know you'll never do it." So much for *gaskiya* in politics.

Amana (trust) in elected officials is also an untenable notion. *Cin amana* (embezzlement) is recognized as a universal practice of civilians in power. As for *ladabi* (appropriate conduct and behavior), the constant insulting, belittling, and abuse (*zage-zage*) heaped upon candidates by each other, in addition to the disrespect shown traditional leaders by opposition party candidates, effectively discredit any semblance of *kirki* (virtue) residing in political actors, or existing within the political process as such.

BARANTAKA AND DEMOCRACY

Even if Nigerian politicians impugned themselves as individuals
by personally violating fundamental Hausa norms of virtue, this
alone does not constitute *systemic* incompatibility between electoral democracy and rural Hausa society. To consider this higher
level of incompatibility, a sketch of traditional Hausa social structure, status, and values is called for.

As M. G. Smith points out, social relations in traditional
Hausa society are manifestations of the principle of *barantaka*-
clientship.[6] An economic and social inferior renders certain services, labor, and efforts to his patron, extends to him deferential
greetings, and informs the patron of any community events which
might affect him. A client, in turn, may expect economic aid (food,
clothing, shelter, farmland) when it is needed or, if he is economically independent, may defer to his patron for advice. But
chapka— allegiance— is a good unto itself, and not directly con-
tingent upon any specific gift or donation. *Barantaka* is the soci-
ological cement which binds political and social unequals to one
another, and channels potentially disruptive inequality into a
stable, self-perpetuating equilibrium.

But who exactly *are* these unequals? Hausa society can be
stratified into several categories, with varying degrees of differentiation. The simplest distinction to make is between nobles
(*sarakuna*) and commoners (*talakawa*). The former include
emirs, chiefs, and their entourage— all those holding hereditary
offices (*masu-sarauta*). *Talakawa* constitute the plebes, the
peasants, the masses— those born to demonstrate respectful
deference to the superior *sarakuna.*

But even among the "non-noble," gradations of social hierarchy amongst the Hausa have been discerned. M. G. Smith claims
that, even without being *sarauta,* the mallamai (Koranic scholars)
possess a social standing just beneath that of the rulers.[7] *Atta-
jirai*— highly successful merchants— also have considerable
daraja , or status. The lowest class amongst the *talakawa,* supposedly, is composed of butchers, drummers, blacksmiths, servants, hunters, and praise-singers. Somewhere in between float
the ordinary farmers, who make up the majority of the people.

When questioned about this textbook definition of their
society, however, villagers in Yardaji took exception to such a
classification. While *sarakuna* might possess greater *iko* (power)
than all others, it was rejected that they therefore had more
daraja (status) than the religious scholars. And farming, a sup-

posedly modest occupational category, was said by villagers to command considerable *daraja*, being the precondition for all survival.

It should not be surprising that a village-eye perspective on social standing and worth might differ from an urban-biased one (of the Smith typology). On many matters, Hausa villagers look askance at city-dwellers and their values, attributing to the city the evils of *laifi*, *wofi*, and *siyasa*— crime, decadence, and politics. (This is especially true in the perception of Kano from Yardaji.) Even though Hausa urbanites are more widely known to look down upon the inhabitants of the *daji* ("bush") for being backward, unsophisticated "country-bumpkins," villagers for their part manifest a moral superiority vis-à-vis their city cousins.

This tension between bush and city (*daji* and *birni*) parallels, to a considerable extent, the duality of tradition and modernity— in Hausa language, the differences between *gargajiya* and *zamani*. While *zamani* ("new times") as such is not condemned in Yardaji (it is, in fact, viewed rather favorably), some of its expressions— including politics— are vigorously criticized. It is crucial here to recognize that *zamani*-related phenomena are not rejected simply because they are "new" or "different," but rather because they pose threats to more fundamental values of the society. Those that pose no such threat are readily integrated.

By way of example, let us examine a "new" value— '*yanci*— which, although not recognized in the classical treatments of Hausa culture and society (e.g., M. G. Smith, Kirk-Greene, Hill), today permeates the ethos and *Weltanschauung* of even the rural Hausa. '*Yanci* may be viewed on two levels, the historico-political and the philosophico-personal. In its first usage, '*yanci* may be translated as "independence." It connotes independence from European rule, sovereignty for Nigeria, and self-determination for the nation. '*Yanci* may also be thought of as "freedom" or "liberty"— freedom from ignorance (*jahilci*), oppression (*zalunci*), and "darkness" (*duhu*). In all its meanings, '*yanci* connotes unambiguously positive changes in the villagers' conception of life, changes that in another context and language are referred to as "decolonization" and "development."

Notwithstanding, despite the acceptability of certain changes in traditional attitudes and aspirations, and despite some ambiguity in stratifying social rank and status on the village level, the hierarchical basis of Hausa social and political relations, as manifested in *barantaka*, remains fundamental. In a lighter or iconoclastic mood, peasants may jokingly refer to the *manya-*

manya— the "big shots," or "fat cats," who have the means to rule, command, and spend— but the legitimacy of their status, prestige, and power (*daraja, girma, iko*) is hardly questioned.

What is more, despite the safety values of upward mobility provided by interclass marriage and *shigege* (achieved, as opposed to inherited, status and occupation), the superiority and privilege of the *manya-manya* are regarded as intrinsic qualities. Class and privilege are not only sanctioned by Hausa society, but are positively valued by *sarakuna* and *talakawa* alike; *daraja, girma*, and *iko* constitute the glue of the Hausa *Gemeinschaft.*

This is not to say that these traditional values cannot be transferred to the secular, or political world. Indeed, Yardaji-ites recognized the elected state governor to be a member of the *sarakuna*, with the requisite degree of *girma* and *iko.* However, the notion that "all men are equal"— the underlying premise of western democratic government— has no equivalent in a society constituted and permeated by *barantaka.* Neither do the precepts "one man, one vote," "popular consent," "majority rule," or "government of the people, by the people, for the people." That a *talaka* has the same knowledge, discernment, and experience as a *sarki*— and therefore merits an equal say in the conduct and composition of government— is a Hausa absurdity. Egalitarianism and equality— the normative founts on which democratic, electoral politics is constructed— lack conceptual as well as linguistic currency in Hausaland. Were they to be introduced, they would probably join that core cluster of values associated with the city, and which, contrasted to those of the bush, might be depicted this way:

A *daraja*-less society— one in which individuals' rank, status, and position are unknown, or disregarded— is the Hausa equivalent of social chaos, or anarchy. According to Yardaji villagers, both *siyasa* and *dimokuradiyya* (politics and democracy) have whittled away at *daraja*, creating a most unfortunate situation. People will tend to do what they want, regardless of their true station and ability, and abandoning respect for legitimate figures of authority.

It is striking how the criticism and distrust of democracy in Hausa Yardaji parallels the critique of that same institution in Plato's Republic:

[I]n democracy . . . there's no compulsion either to exercise authority if you are capable of it, or to submit to authority if you

Normative Clusters as Perceived in Yardaji

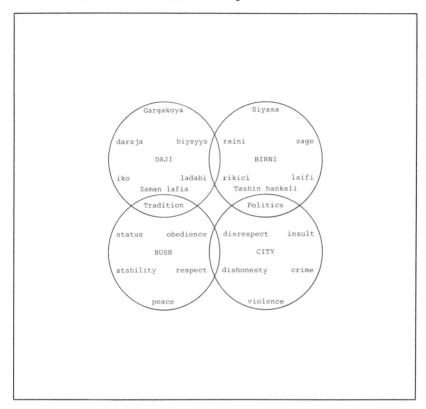

don't want to . . . ; democracy with a grandiose gesture sweeps all [principles] away and doesn't mind what the habits and background of its politicians are, provided they profess themselves the people's friends. . . . It's an . . . anarchic form of society . . . which treats all men as equal, whether they are equal or not.[8]

Hassan Haruna, a herder in Yardaji, vividly described "democracy" in more concrete and culturally felicitous terms. In democracy, he said, "men wander around like cattle, without any direction. They make all kinds of excited noises, but there's no sense to it. Each goes his own way, lost, until there's no more herd." This is not the judgment of a *sarki*, or chief, nor that of an aspiring philosopher-king. It is rather the view of most *talakawa*, ordinary Hausa villagers whose powers of human observation and creative analogy may rival the persuasive capacities of even the most silver-tongued "son of politics" (*dan siyasa*).

CHAPTER SEVEN

Campaign Rallies

Perhaps no single political event so impressed the inhabitants of Yardaji as the rallies and speeches conducted throughout the electoral campaign. Due to its modest size, the village itself did not host the visit of any major candidate; nevertheless, Yardaji's relative proximity to Zango (eight miles) and Daura (twenty miles) did allow villagers to see and hear major political figures, including the nation's president himself, Alhaji Shehu Shagari. Nigerian political rallies, at least in the Northern "bush," took on the dual character of western populist politicking along with fundamentalist Islamic (and African) rites and symbols. In the absence of television, and given the limited impact of newspapers or tracts (apart from the schoolteachers, villagers read little besides the Koran), personal campaigning took on even greater significance than had these phenomena been present.

Despite the self-proclaimed differences among the parties, the *form* of their political rallies, at least in Daura emirate, was remarkably similar. Of course, all had their fair share of party posters, tee-shirts, and even bumper stickers. But it is in the campaign rallies themselves that the distinctive nature of Nigerian politicking was most clearly seen. It was as if there had emerged an accepted, even institutionalized, way of campaigning, and deviation from the model might have smacked of unprofessionalism, in the eyes of the people. In the bush, moreover, campaign rallies represented, above all, a form of entertainment for small townsmen and neighboring villagers. Adult males and boys flocked to attend as many of the rallies as possible, regardless of their personal partisan preference.

The typical campaign rally began with a caravan of minibuses, filled with chanting and singing supporters brought from other areas of the state, and blaring party songs from loudspeakers rigged to the vehicles. (The GNPP caravan in Zango was inaugurated by a local youth doing motorcycle stunts on the road leading to, and through, the town.) The candidate would then arrive, waving and smiling, and immediately proceed, in his vehicle, to the palace of the town's traditional ruler (the *sarki*, or emir, in the case of Daura; the *hakimi*, or district head, in the case of Zango). There, a private audience (attended by the appropriate courtiers and advisers) would be held between the candidate and the traditional ruler.

The substance of the audience between candidate and traditional ruler was not made known to the public outside; paying one's immediate respect to the traditional chief is a *sine qua non* in Hausa politesse, and by no means the affair of the community at large. (In the case of President Shagari's meeting with the emir of Daura, a local government member present reported that the president made a speech on the necessity of conducting the elections peacefully.) The candidate would then proceed to the center of town, where the formal presentation to the public would actually begin.

Invariably, the rally would begin with traditional Islamic prayers, led by a venerable *limam* (priest) of the community. (The *limam* would have been introduced by the rally's "warm-up" speaker.) It is significant that even the most "radical" parties—particularly the People's Redemption Party and the Nigerian People's Party—took particular pains to demonstrate their traditionalism and religiosity on this score.

The "warm-up" speaker would return to the podium to introduce the candidate. Before making any statement, however, the speaker would engage the crowd in *responsa*, by shouting the party name or slogan and having the crowd shout back the appropriate response. Thus, a GNPP speaker would begin by shouting "GNPP!" and have the crowd roar back "*Adalci*!" ("Justice!"). After this was done several times, the speaker would then shout the response (e.g., "*Adalci*!"), and the crowd would take up the original call (e.g., "GNPP!"). So popular was this *responsa* method of audience participation that persons who had absolutely no intention of voting for the party in question nevertheless joined—and quite enthusiastically—in the chanting.

NPP was perhaps the most adept at audience animation, attracting crowds through its catchy *responsa*:

(Speaker)	"NPP!"
(Crowd)	"Canji!" ("Change!")
(S)	"NPP!"
(C)	"Canji!"
(S)	"Canji!"
(C)	"Dolle!" ("It's necessary!")
(S)	"Canji!"
(C)	"Dolle!"
(S)	"Dolle!"
(C)	"NPP!"

This warm-up speaker would then introduce a local party member of the community (i.e., Zango or Daura), who, after invoking the *responsa* litany, would make a short speech about party unity. (Participation of a "local boy" was immensely popular with the crowd.) The warm-up speaker would then launch into a fervent introduction of the actual candidate, who would finally mount the podium.

The candidate began with the obligatory party *responsa*. (By this time, most of the audience had caught on to the lines, and heartily shouted them back. The most vocal and animated group in all the rally crowds, incidentally, were teenage and preadolescent boys— in other words, those who were too young to vote.) A typical speech of the opposition parties had the candidate hold up a box of Omo detergent, ask the crowd how much it had cost four years prior, and how much it cost then. Price rises for this and other consumer commodities (e.g., soap, kerosene, batteries) were then laid at the doorstep of the incumbent NPN party.

Having invoked the negative qualities of the present regime, the candidate would then promise the people water pumps, electricity, jobs, medicine, education. Some candidates would try to outdo the other parties by making even more extravagant promises (such as NPP's pledge to plant a wall of trees along the six-hundred-mile border with Niger, to "keep out" the Sahara Desert), but generally candidates invoked the more established needs of the people. They also always took care to make reference to the "historic" importance of Zango (or Daura), and emphasize (if such were the case) how their rival(s) did not think enough of the town to visit it.

Throughout a speech, traditional praise-singers (*maroka*) would heap blessings and praises upon the candidate for his greatness, grace, and generosity. And, in accordance with Hausa Islamic custom, any statement of future will, intent, and activity would be qualified by the traditional Hausa formula, *in Allah yarda* ("God willing"). (For example, the GNPP warm-up speaker in Zango introduced his candidate in this way: "And now, the [next] Governor of Kaduna—God willing—Alhaji Sabiu Nuhu!") Candidates would wind up their public rallies in the same spirit in which they began—with reference to God's support for their party, with blessings, and with prayers.

Due to its historic, rather unique character, President Shagari's campaign visit to Daura (on July 29, 1983) merits specific mention.

As with any head of state of a major power, Shagari traveled under considerable police protection. His visit to the emir's palace was noted by thousands of cheering onlookers, who were no less impressed with the president's bodyguards than with the president himself. It was with the emir that Shagari expressed his overriding concern for peaceful elections.

Shagari's warm-up speaker, in the field outside the old city, savagely lambasted the president's major opponents. Awolowo, he claimed, had incited violence in the 1959 elections, and was anti-North; Azikiwe he denounced for his role as Nigerian president in 1966, when the country began to experience its "troubles."

It was by their sheer presence, more than their words, that the NPN speakers attested to the broad-based, interethnic, transregional, interreligious, and even bi-gender image that the National Party of Nigeria was attempting to project. Given that the Daura audience was itself exceedingly homogeneous—Muslim, Hausa, and male—NPN's ecumenicalism was all the more significant.

NPN's campaign *responsa*, of which each speaker invoked at least a part, ran like this:

(Speaker)	"NPN!"
(Crowd)	"Aminci!" ("Friendship!")
(S)	"Aminci!"
(C)	"NPN!"
(S)	"Shehu!"

(C)   "Shagari!"
(S)   "Shagari!"
(C)   "In '83!"

Occasionally, the official party slogan ("One Party! One Nation!") was attempted as a *responsa*, but this overtaxed the linguistic capability of the non-English-speaking crowd.

One of the keynote speakers was an impressive Yoruba, who spoke, in English, against Awolowo. Virtually no one could understand what he said, due to the language barrier, but the audience enthusiastically responded as if it did, by verbally acknowledging words that it could recognize (such as "NPN" or "Shagari").

The Daura crowd was even more bemused by the next speaker— a woman, who addressed them in both Yoruba and Hausa. This speaker touched off general laughter when she addressed herself to both men *and* women attending the rally: inasmuch as women in traditional Hausa society are "exclud[ed] from the system . . . which governs the political relations of men,"[1] the only females present were young girls selling snacks. But being addressed by both a Yoruba man and a Yoruba *woman* certainly provoked no resentment among the Daura populace, who rather seemed to enjoy the originality of the event.

When Shehu Shagari himself took the podium, he raised the major theme of his campaign, thus invoking a major pillar of Hausa culture: *zaman lafiya*, or peace. He belittled the other parties in a crowd-engaging way, rhetorically asking, "Do any of you know what *canji* means? Or which party talks of it?" He accused NPP (to which he was referring) of having no religion and of being anti-Islamic.

Interestingly, Shagari chose this rally to invoke the threat of communism, an ideology quite remote from the consciousness of the people in Daura emirate. He used the Hausa word *gurguzu*, which literally means a "crowd of persons of same type," and linked it to the NPP. ("Everything is the same, and all mixed up.") The incumbent president concluded with the necessity of preserving the traditional values of *gargajiya* and *addini*— tradition and religion.

Closer to Yardaji, and perhaps most politically savvy of all, was the PRP campaign rally for gubernatorial candidate Musa Musawa. Of all the parties that campaigned in Zango, PRP was the most impressive and, for the participants, the most exciting. Dispensing with the usual roll call of long speeches, preceded by (also long) warm-up speeches, the crux of the PRP rally was its catchy campaign jingle, whose chorus many in the audience knew and sang: "*PRP nasara siyasa/Tana cika alkawari garemu.*" ("*PRP is the politics of success/It keeps its promises to us.*")

The singing was eventually accompanied by drummers, giving the PRP the most African, or at least Hausa, flavor of all the rallies. Party supporters, including women, had arrived in a minibus caravan, and all wore colorful PRP costumes. When the candidate finally did speak, he gave a fiery, sarcastic, and witty speech. He criticized Shagari for traveling to the North by airplane, and being chauffeured around by limousine, but not visiting Zango—whereas he, Musa Musawa, *had* indeed come (even if by minibus) all the way to Zango. He drew laughs by calling Abba Musa Rimi, the incumbent state governor, the "big-lipped" one, and engaged in other *zage* (insults) against his rivals. But for all the contentious, rebellious rhetoric, Musa closed his talk on a traditional note, saying that it was time, as dusk was setting in, for everyone to go to his *mallam* (religious leader) and say the evening prayers.

The campaign rallies that Yardaji-ites attended, as the above accounts demonstrate, represented tangible syncretisms of new political forms with traditional social values. *Siyasa*— politics— meant crowds, loudspeakers, and minibuses; it meant posters, tee-shirts; vans and Volkswagens; strange languages and "liberated" women, animation, excitement. Electoral politics, U.S.-style, meant a new Nigeria—but a new Nigeria with a question mark.

At the same time, in their rural campaign, all the parties took care to co-opt, or at least not alienate, the fundamental sociocultural pillar of the Northern peasantry: Islam. When they went into the countryside, even "radical" parties bowed to custom by paying their respects to traditional rulers. The dominant NPN went even further, by appealing directly to the traditional values of a conservative, rural-minded, Hausa society: *zaman lafiya, gargajiya, aminci*— peace, tradition, friendship. It was *not* an ethnic appeal, however, so much as a cultural one. Yardaji-ites who supported NPN did so not because it was a "Hausa party" but because it incarnated the villagers' values of tradition and stability.

An unrecognized paradox was that the government was advocating, in effect, a fairly revolutionary (for Hausa peasants) means—the ballot—for a relatively conservative end—the maintenance of the status quo, including the traditional chieftaincy.

Villagers were being urged to vote to maintain a system whose underlying principle was their own subordination (as *talakawa*) to the *sarakuna*: a democratic means for an anti-egalitarian end.

But it was not this sociopolitical paradox that bothered the people of Yardaji, nor disillusioned them concerning the role or value of electoral politics. Most villagers valued traditional institutions, including the chieftaincy, and saw nothing inconsistent with voting that way. What did alienate them, however, was the repugnant antisocial behavior that all parties and politicians seemed to indulge in, and which became identified with politics itself: *zage-zage*, the ceaseless, scathing heaping of insult and abuse upon one's competitors, rivals, and adversaries. Nowhere was *zage-zage* so institutionalized as in the songs that party-singers sang.

CHAPTER EIGHT

Songs of Insult

Songs and poems have long been associated with government in Hausaland. In the old days of traditional rule, professional *maroka* (praise-singers) earned handsome "gifts" by publicly lauding, complimenting, and flattering wealthy or powerful benefactors. Traditionally, *maroka* occupied a relatively low rung on the Hausa ladder of social status (*cf.* M. G. Smith, 1959), and were content with the few shillings of naira that their patrons would give them. The gush of oil and the return of politics in the 1970s, however, dramatically elevated the potential reward of well-connected praise-singers, and hence their stature and significance.

But the patron, too, earns enormous prestige in lavishly rewarding the praise-singer. It is not only a matter of encouraging further expressions of support by professional "image-makers." The more a *manya-manya* gives away, the more his reputation of greatness in the eyes of the public is enhanced. An image of *arziki, daraja,* and *karamci*— wealth, status, and generosity— goes a long way in generating awe and admiration among Hausa *talakawa.* In a political context, the money that a Nigerian politician gives away in public to a *maroki* may be considered the equivalent of the U.S. candidate's investment in media advertising: both expenditures aim to "buy" favorable publicity for the spender. But whereas political commercials in the United States cease after elections, victorious Nigerian candidates must substantiate their "greatness" continually, even after their accession to office.

By way of example, the 1983 festivities of Daura, celebrating the holiday of Mawludi, may be invoked. Joining the emir of Daura and his court were many high-ranking state officers, including the governor of Kaduna state himself. For a single song exalting the governor, a praise-singer was rewarded with a motorcycle. (Someone else contributed five hundred naira for "gas money.") Other praise-singers were given one or even two hundred naira for their lyrics. At one point, five-naira notes were thrown from an overhead balustrade to the praise-singers' area, provoking a scramble for the bills that pitted even policemen against *maroka.*

It is worth noting that these events occurred in December 1983, or four months after the governor had been elected, and one month before the military coup d'état. Even in office, with four years to serve, social *cum* political custom obliged officeholders to continue the public manifestations of prestige-building that characterized the campaign period. The source or legitimacy of this political capital was rarely questioned, even though such "gifts" obviously exceeded the official salaries that the officeholders were allotted. It was precisely this kind of profligate public behavior, especially at a time of national economic crisis, which provoked the military to step in and put an end to civilian "democracy." From a cultural point of view, the expansion of electoral politics to Northern Nigeria thus not only exaggerated and distorted otherwise justifiable traditional Hausa norms of status-enhancement (e.g., *karamci*) by their incorporation into the political process, but virtually assured their corruption.

Electoral politics in Nigeria also entailed a further corruption in the traditional use and value of Hausa praise-singing and praise-singers. Whereas, traditionally, *maroka* were positive forces of praise or social criticism, partisan competition bestowed on them a new, and negative, function: vulgar depreciation of their patrons' rivals. In Hausa terminology, they moved from being singers of *roka* (praise) to being agents of *zage* (insult).

The extension of Hausa song to the realm of politics is by no means new. As early as the beginning of the century, anti-western sentiment, and the corrupting influence of European ways, was expressed in lyrics:

I assure you that I will not stay to follow Nasara [Christians].
They are too bothersome, and they have bad intentions.
To destroy the religion of the Muslims, Nasara.
There are many hypocrites among us,
Who value highly the ways of Nasara.[1]

By the time independence approached, tension between
(Christian) British and (Muslim) Hausa was replaced by suspicion between northern and southern Nigerians. Debate over the type of sovereign Nigeria should take was likewise reflected in song:

There is disagreement over what is wanted,
As to the way Nigeria should be governed.
The aim of the South, if they are empowered,
Is to turn the whole land into a republic.
As for us, our aim is to divide,
So the North can choose monarchical government
Understand the aim of monarchical government
And the many dangers of a republican government
The King and houses of parliament,
And law, that's monarchical government.
The government of representatives, all mixed up,
No king, no queen, only policemen, only soldiers, order,
That is republican government.[2]

Even where criticism against rulers was deemed legitimate, it was expressed by invoking social and religious norms— but certainly not personal insult.

Then emirs, you should accumulate wealth,
By fair, not by dishonest means.
You should look on the beard of your brother,
Which is burning and struggling
So you can look for water and sprinkle it,
So that yours too will not suffer.
If you will follow without caring
The ways of the men who had gone before
You will sing that song of "had-I-known
I would have taken the advice of Gaskiya."
May God forbid that you should say so
And protect the whole of the North![3]

By 1983, however, and encouraged by the freewheeling political atmosphere of the Second Republic, campaign-singers broke beyond the bounds of acceptable social criticism and engaged in outright *zage-zage*.[4] The following extracts were taken from pre-

taped cassettes that were available in Daura and broadcast to
people throughout the emirate.

> Who went to Togo, drank beer, and grabbed a woman?
> He grabbed her buttocks, she said "Stop it, old man!"
> He said, "Wait, listen, I'm President of Nigeria."
> The President of Nigeria, who absconds with the nation's money—
> But now NPN nominates him candidate—
> To hell with you niggardly ones!
> Our "teachers" are whiskey drunkards.
> We've had enough of you
> "Our whiskey "leaders," we say to you,
> "God is enough for us."
>
> —*NPP campaign song*

> Every slimy [NPP] supporter is a dog.
> If he dies, do not bury him.
> Burn him in fire, the ingrate dog!
> Jatau [i.e., Governor Rimi of Kano] is a slave to the Jews.
> He will teach your sons to become effeminate
> They will tie women's wrappers round their hips.
> He treats people like dirt.
> Kano has . . . elected a consummate hypocrite.
> May God take away this Satan,
> King of the Ingrates.
>
> —*NPN campaign song*

Ridiculing the NPN symbol, a house with corn growing round
it, PRP singers mocked:

> Here is a house with a poster.
> Look, what is the symbol?
> They drew a house without a gate,
> With corn sprouting a "beard" [i.e., fiber on the ear].
> An ear of corn is shameless.
> Like a child, it is carried on its mother's back,
> But it sprouts a beard.
> Now if that isn't the height of shamelessness,
> To sprout a beard on your mother's back.
> It is madness and nonsense to have corn as a symbol.
> We shall pluck the corn, break its ear, throw it into the fire,and burn
>   the beard.
> Don't be ensnared by the enemy,
> Traitors of the people, traitors of our country!

The depths to which rival parties sank to vilify one another
in both speech and song could not but discredit *siyasa* (politics)
in the eyes of a community raised on *kirki, ladabi,* and *mutunci*

(virtue, politesse, and self-respect). But *siyasa*, by virtue of being part of Nigeria, remained a national phenomenon that Yardaji-ites could not dismiss entirely. For better or worse, Yardaji was part of Nigeria; Nigeria, in 1983, meant political campaigns; and political campaigns meant systematic *zage-zage.* Faced with an inescapable situation that pitted national pressures against cultural norms, the Hausa villagers of Yardaji had little choice but to go along, but they did so with an understandably jaded view of the *dimokuradiyya* (democracy) the elections were supposed to represent.

It would be naive, however, to suppose that the most recent banishment of electoral politics in Nigeria means that traditional Hausa culture and morality in places like Yardaji are whole again. Politics in the bush has had a deleterious impact on the consciousness of the peasantry, an impact that may not be capable of measurement but is nonetheless real. The extent to which the "democratic experiment" in Nigeria has made inroads against these norms and values constituting the backbone of village social life should not be underestimated. It should also illuminate—especially to those wishing to "export democracy"—the price that such experiments can carry in terms of cultural integrity and social cohesion, especially for those rural, peripheral groups that tend to be vulnerable, anyway, to processes emanating from the center. To regard a "democratic experiment" as a scientist might a chemical experiment—where initial failure is merely followed by a "second try" (perhaps with adjusted variables)—blithely ignores the repercussions that such "experiments" may have on their involuntary guinea pigs. This goes beyond saying that U.S.-style politics may be "inadapted" to certain Third World settings. A common refrain echoed time and time again by Yardaji-ites, especially when discussing politics, elections, and civilian government, is *Nijeriya ta lalaci*— "Nigeria has been ruined." Putting aside the objective validity of such a statement, its mere expression, by ordinary, apolitical Hausa *talakawa*, raises a more disturbing prospect: the potentially destabilizing effect of modern electoral democracy upon indigenous, peasant-based communities and cultures.

CHAPTER NINE

Chiefs and the Campaign

In a dual polity, run by an electoral multi-party system and also by an inherited, traditional chieftaincy, what is the role of traditional chiefs in secular (i.e., national) elections? As we have shown in Chapter 2, this question, as it relates to Nigeria's First Republic, is thoroughly examined in C. S. Whitaker's work, *The Politics of Tradition: Continuity and Change in Northern Nigeria*, where Whitaker demonstrates the direct, and preponderant, influence of the Hausa and Fulani *sarakuna* in Northern Nigeria elections and politics. Here, as it relates to the Second Republic, our aim is similar if more limited in scope: to examine the role, attitudes, and activities of at least two traditional rulers—the chief of Yardaji and the emir of Daura—during the 1983 campaign. The major conclusion to be drawn is that, while the influence of traditional chiefs in electoral politics has certainly not been eradicated, between the 1960s and the 1980s there has been a marked erosion in their political clout, and a corresponding secularization of the political process. Whether this political secularization enhanced the credibility and legitimacy of electoral democracy in the eyes of the *talakawa*, however, is another matter entirely. In fact, based on the beliefs and opinions of most Yardaji-ites, one might argue that the widening rift between *sarakai na siyasa* and *sarakai na gargajiya* (that is, the separation of powers between political and traditional leaders)—which is itself a cornerstone of modern politics—has actually tended to delegitimize and to discredit notions of "democracy" and "politics" for these same *talakawa*. Furthermore, *both* institutions—the

88

chieftaincy as well as democratic politics— have suffered as a result, highlighting another potential price of misguided political "experiments" for peasants in the bush.

In Nigeria's First Republic, traditional rulers— continuing in the British colonial tradition of Indirect Rule— were allowed, if not actually encouraged, to serve as the people's representatives in the new nation's modern (parliamentary) political institutions. The fact that, at least in the North, the *sarakuna* used their traditional prestige and status with the *talakawa* to extend their sphere of influence to post-independence civilian government was not lost upon Nigeria's post-1966 military leaders, perhaps the most secularizing force within the Nigerian society.[1] Accordingly, when drawing up the new constitution that was to define and regulate the transition to civilian rule, the military government of Lt. Gen. Olusegun Obasanjo officially excluded traditional rulers— who in Nigeria are on government payroll and thus quasi-civil servants— from membership in both the national and state Houses of Assembly: "No person shall be qualified for election to the Senate or the House of Representatives [or a House of Assembly] if . . . he is a person employed in the public service of the Federation or of any state."

Moreover, traditional rulers were explicitly prohibited from active campaigning on behalf of any candidate or party. Significantly, this divorce of traditional rulers from partisan politicking was acknowledged across the board, by village peasants and chiefs alike: *gargajiya da ban, siyasa da ban*— "Traditional rule is one thing, politics is another." And yet while acknowledging the superior *iko* (power) of secular (i.e., political) institutions and government over traditional ones, the *legitimacy* of such politicians and secular office-holders lagged behind that of the *sarakuna na gargajiya*. As the chief of Yardaji rightly pointed out, "Politicians come and go — even a Governor may be thrown out, or replaced after a few years— but traditional leaders exist forever." Even without prescience of the impending coup, the *dagacin Yardaji* thus succinctly contrasted the instability of regimes and personalities of the secular political system with the continuity, longevity, and hence greater legitimacy of the traditional institutions. Even if subordinate to state government in terms of its immediate scope and exercise of power, the chieftaincy in Hausaland serves as a psychological as well as cultural "back-up" support system, when secular modes of government in the country do break down— as they are wont to do, periodically.

Alhaji Haruna, village chief of Yardaji, is fully aware of the demarcation between secular and traditional government. Head of the *gunduma* (village area) of Yardaji for three decades, he has also had experience as *dan majalisa* (representative) and *wakili* (deputy) in the local Daura government—this, at a time when the only way to get to Daura was by horse. (Today the chief owns a Peugeot pickup truck.) "But these days" (he explained in June 1983) "no traditional leader may enter, or have anything to do, with politics." He admitted he didn't know why this was so: "Those who made the rules [and wrote the constitution], they know their reasons." As *mai-gari* and *dagaci* (village and village area chief), Alhaji Haruna neither campaigned nor overtly expressed his political preferences to the village as a whole. Circumspectly, he expressed his opinion that NPN would prevail in the elections, but, at least in public, he went no further in forecasting the results.

This is not to say *mai-gari* was personally uninterested in the elections—especially since his own son was NPN candidate for the Zango district seat in the Kaduna state House of Assembly. By way of transistor radio (and periodic visits by his son, the *kantoma* of Zango), the chief keenly followed developments in both the national and local campaigns. As far as political happenings in Yardaji itself, however, *mai-gari* remained curiously aloof. He did not know, for instance, who was the village representative for each of the parties, let alone the intricacies of party organization, campaign strategies, or "decampings" (i.e., leaving one party for another). Despite his undisputed authority in the village over virtually all other matters, ranging from the legal to the marital, the chief of Yardaji did keep a deliberately low profile as concerned village partisan politics throughout the entire electoral campaign.

In the case of the emir, however, the "apolitical" nature of the chieftaincy was much more ambiguous. In the week prior to the presidential elections, the emir of Daura went on *rangadi,* on "bush-tour," throughout his emirate, ostensibly to encourage participation in the upcoming elections. He did not explicitly lobby for any one party or candidate, for this would have been to overstep the proper bounds of his role and authority as traditional leader—but for those who wished to "listen between the lines," a more subtle message may have been heard.

The emir was accompanied during his tours by representatives of both the traditional and secular sectors: the district head (*hakimi*), village area heads (*dagatai*), and ward heads (*masu-ungowyi*) throughout the Zango distinct were all in attendance, flanked by traditional palace guards (*dogarai*) and three policemen (including a sergeant) from the Nigerian police force. After a preliminary proclamation was shouted to the assembled villagers (to set the "agenda" for the present meeting), the emir himself— sitting on the only chair present— spoke. (Except for the *dogarai* and policemen, everyone else sat on the ground. The notables— district and village area heads— were provided mats for their comfort and station; commoners squatted on the earth.)

The emir, with his usual courtesy, began by thanking the assembled people for their presence. (Even such a seemingly innocuous beginning is not without significance, for it betokens a far cry from an older, more "autocratic" image of a Hausa *sarki*. While no question of egalitarianism between *sarki* and *talaka* is brooked, such courtesies do create a heightened sense of *mutunci*, or self-respect, among ordinary villagers.)

He is touring everywhere, the emir said, to deliver this talk. But the people should know that he is doing it with authorization (*umurni*), and that it was not his idea alone. (This, in all probability, was a reference to the president of Nigeria, who had paid a courtesy call to the emir's palace during his recent campaign trip to Daura.)

The emir urged *hakuri* (patience, forbearance) on the part of the people during the elections. "Politics is not a matter of insults or abuse [*zage*], nor craziness [*hauka*], nor shameless behavior [*rishin kunya*], nor treachery [*wulakanta*]." The people should know this, and maintain themselves with dignity, and "patience." Politicians commit the sin of insulting others, even if indirectly; but the people should ignore this kind of behavior. The people— the commoners— know that they are with their chiefs; this is where their respect, their loyalty, should go. The emir prayed— and this was the major theme of his intercession throughout the campaign— that the elections would pass in peace, and without any fighting.

They— the people— should elect the person who will give them work, and who rules well. Then, in detail, he elaborated upon the procedures of the elections, and the order in which they would take place (presidential, gubernatorial, senatorial, congressional, and state representative). Commenting on the presidential contest, the emir explained:

> This will be an election from Lagos to Kongolam [i.e., the length of the country], and will be held all in one day. If those in the South elect the one they want, the North will not be electing the one *they*

want. Inevitably, the Southerners will then rule. Because of this,
everyone should come out and vote. If Igbos and Yorubas come out
and vote, they will elect *their* man. If Hausas, and Fulanis, don't
vote, then necessarily the Igbos or Yorubas will rule. This is why
everyone should come out, to vote for the one who is close to him
[*Kowa da kowa ya fito, ya yi zabe wanda ya kusa da shi*].

In graphic and personal terms, the emir inveighed on the entire people to participate in the elections: "Each and every one
must come out and vote— fathers and sons, husbands and wives,
old men and old women, lepers and the blind. . . ."

Using analogies to which all peasants can relate— adages
drawn from farming— the emir impressed upon the audience the
necessity of making the right choice:

> What you sow is what you shall reap [*Abin da ka shuka, shi za ya
>   fito*]. If you plant millet, will groundnuts grow?
> [The assembled responded: "No."]
> If you transplant sugar cane, will you get melon in its place?
> ["No."]
> So it is with people's character, that which you choose now is what
>   you will see in the future.

Changing analogy, but not method, the emir continued: "In
the old days, people fought with swords, and spears, and bows
and arrows. But now, this time has passed. Now, it is with ballot that one fights. . . ." Reemphasizing the importance of the vote,
and the necessity of accepting the outcome, the emir went on:
"Voting is not wrestling, it is not boxing. If someone is thrown
down, that's it, you don't keep on fighting."

Before leaving the crowd for Baure, where he would repeat
his message, the emir said that he wished "health, peace, and
friendship" (*lafiya da zaman lafiya da aminci*) upon all assembled. The meeting concluded with traditional Muslim prayers
(addu'a).

As the narration demonstrates, the emir appears to have
faithfully discharged his duty to encourage electoral participation in a relatively nonpartisan manner. No parties were mentioned by name, just as no particular candidates were singled out
for either disapproval or praise. Even if the emir did exhibit a degree of regionalist preference (in invoking the possibility of a
"southern" electoral victory), it was more to incite the peasants
to vote in the first place than anything else. In Daura, at least,
no "heavy hand" of traditional ruler electioneering, of the kind

reputedly rampant during the First Republic, appears to have been operating.

For those familiar with the particularities of the 1983 campaign, however, other, more subtle partisan messages *were* being conveyed to the Daura voters. It was no secret that the populistic campaign themes and tactics of at least two of the parties— PRP and NPP—displeased not only the more moderate NPN supporters but the traditional chieftaincy as a whole. Veiled references to "insults," "craziness," and "shameless behavior" brought to mind the crowds of undisciplined NPP or PRP youths crying out for "Power!" and "Change!" or the unrestrained, sometime virulent speeches and songs by members of these opposition parties.

The emir's personal preference for the more moderate, pro-establishment and pro-chieftaincy NPN could not have been a secret to any Daura *talaka*. His assertion that the "people are with their chiefs" is significant in this regard, as is his reference to the "authority" to conduct such meetings. Without once mentioning the name of Shehu Shagari, the emir indirectly summoned the incumbent president to mind, in his calls for a "patient," "peaceful," and "dignified" approach to politics. His choice of symbolism—especially his agricultural analogies—instilled a sense of caution and conservatism in electoral matters, an ethic not to be lightly dismissed by the subsistence-level, small-scale farmers. Even the emir's vocabulary contained certain code words and phrases; *zaman lafiya* and *aminci* ("peace" and "friendship"), which the emir invoked in concluding the assembly, are not only high moral virtues in Hausa culture but served as the official slogans for Shagari's National Party of Nigeria.

Whether the emir's subtle message to the villagers throughout Daura emirate strictly violated the partisan neutrality of traditional leaders in electoral politics is a complicated matter to judge. It is perhaps more significant, however, that the politicking that did go on *was* subtle and indirect. In the case of Daura—as conservative and traditional an emirate as the Hausa North gets—the people were *not* instructed whom to vote for, in any straightforward, unequivocal way. Even if the traditional chiefs were not completely depoliticized in terms of partisan preferences (and few would suggest that such is ever completely possible), their deliberate, conscious efforts to contain their partisan wishes, and *not* unduly foist them upon their peasant subjects, is more significant than whatever lapses in this regard did occur. It represents an evolving tendency, in the face of earlier electoral practice, for the traditional chieftaincy not only to recognize the line separating secular from traditional politics but to respect it. Whether this role differentiation on the part of the traditional chieftaincy stems from an increasing sense of civic obedience, or, rather, fear of sanctions, is another matter entirely. In fact, given the inherent instability, jaded legitimacy, and dubitable longevity of civilian, "modern" politics in Nigeria, it may be argued that, in a certain way, traditional leaders' credibility is in fact *enhanced*, in the eyes of the people, the more they do distance themselves from secular, partisan, and electoral politics. Certainly, this claim may be supported as concerns the emir of Daura and the chief of Yardaji.

CHAPTER TEN

Voting in the Bush

An atmosphere of insouciance, rather than a preoccupation with *Realpolitik*, normally pervades daily life in Yardaji. The aura surrounding at least the first of the five elections, however, injected a tone of collective seriousness in the village that was not to be reexperienced until the coup d'état, still more than four months away.

While even the slightest suggestion of political violence in the village would have been ludicrous, local authorities in nearby Daura dutifully followed official government instructions to ensure "security." Two fully equipped policemen,[1] replete with kit bags, helmets, and rifles, were thus dispatched to maintain "law and order" in the village. In placid Yardaji, it was the presence of these uniformed, armed "visitors" that raised the anxiety level far beyond what the voting itself might have done. It was also widely known that orders had been issued to arrest anyone near the voting stations who was not there to vote or to serve in an official supervisory capacity.

There were nine official polling stations, located at the two primary schools on the eastern and western edges of the village. (In addition, there was one polling station in the outlying bush, outside of Yardaji.) At each station, there were village representatives from each of the parties to witness the proceedings and the eventual tallying, in addition to two officially designated presiding officers. These were generally secondary school students or primary school teachers, themselves hailing from the village. (The Federal Election Commission, or FEDECO, had or-

"Guarding" the polling stations in Yardaji: James Ahida and Moses Bodi, of the Nigerian police force, in riot gear (Voting in Yardaji was conducted in characteristic tranquility.)

ganized workshops for polling agents and officers in the weeks preceding the elections.) Large posters explaining voting procedures— and penalties for electoral offenses— were posted on the schoolhouse walls near the voting booths. This, however, was merely *pro forma*; not only was all FEDECO literature printed in *Turanci* (English, but literally "European"), and thus incomprehensible to the overwhelming majority of villagers, but it was written in a highly formal, legalistic jargon that would confound any villager who possessed even a rudimentary mastery of the language.[2]

August 1983 was smack in the middle of Northern Nigeria's rainy season and also in the height of the region's single annual agricultural season. Planting had been completed two months earlier, and harvesting would not begin until late September. Election time, therefore, was also the moment for crucial weeding and crop care, lest the millet and sorghum stalks become stunted, or the peanut yield puny and sparse. For the villagers, it was more important, without a doubt, to be weeding in Yardaji's fields of millet than in Nigeria's garden of politics.

Nevertheless, they voted. And because of the fieldwork that was waiting, they voted early. They formed lines behind each polling station, and were subdued in a way normally reserved for inoculations and funeral services. By 9:00 A.M., a large proportion of the men had already voted; women arrived at the polling stations later, and, careful to avoid even moderate contact with the men, spontaneously formed an unofficial "women's only" line. Between late morning and late afternoon, the hottest part of the day, voting activity was virtually nil.

Fulanis living in the bush outside the village straggled in throughout the day, many of them walking considerable distances to get to their designated polling station in Yardaji. Since FEDECO had decreed that the polls were to close at 6:00 P.M. sharp, not a few would-be voters made the trip in vain; even if some villagers knew how to tell time, fewer had the means to do so. (This is particularly true in the case of the women; it is unusual for a woman to possess a watch.)

Applying chronometric rules in a society whose time-telling capability is sun-dependent is not the only example of official Nigeria's contextually inappropriate administration. We have already mentioned that FEDECO "communicated" using a language and method totally alien to the overwhelming majority of the villagers (i.e., pin-up posters in English legalese). Mention should also be made of the seemingly inappropriate, if not arbitrary, fixing of the voting age.

If few adults in Yardaji use a watch to keep track of time, virtually none know their true age. Older people date themselves according to the famines they were born in, or between; only schoolchildren will dare to approximate their age within a margin of error less than ten years. Girls are usually married by the time they are fourteen or fifteen, and boys, even if they must wait somewhat longer (so they can accumulate a suitable dowry), are treated as adults in terms of both work and legal responsibility, long before they become husbands. In short, villagers just do not know how old they are and, because it does not matter, hardly care.

Upon this system of age-grade classification, where persons assume early (by western standards) moral and legal majority, the framers of Nigeria's Second Republic constitution applied a seemingly foreign standard of legal and civil competence: "109.— (2) Every citizen of Nigeria, who has attained the age of 18 years residing in Nigeria at the time of the registration of voters for purposes of election to any legislative house, shall be entitled to register as a voter for that election." Section 124.— (5) invoked this same voting age provision for "election to the office of President."

Even if there were a means to determine a potential voter's true age, the adoption of an eighteen-year-old age requirement hardly reflects the social and legal reality of either rural or urban

Hausa (and probably most African) life. As relates to the actual impact upon the 1983 Nigerian elections, the system "erred" on the side of liberality: in Yardaji alone, barely adolescent boys and girls were enfranchised, and Nigerian television itself reportedly filmed even younger children in line to vote.[3] But the point is not merely the difficulty in establishing or inferring a selected age requirement in an "ageless" cultural environment, but rather the specious rationality of applying western-derived maturation standards in a traditional African culture and society. To Nigerians like those of Yardaji, the association of "democracy" with somewhat alien notions of precision and procedure (e.g., 6:00 A.M. poll closing, a voting age of eighteen years, "European" legal instruction)—even if (or perhaps because) impossible to implement—could only further the perceived distance between the politics (*siyasa*) of the outside and the norms and values (*gargajiya*) of the community.

But just what did voting in Yardaji entail? And how many villagers (especially the women) actually knew what they were doing?

A voter would hand his or her registration card (issued several months previously) to the polling station agent, at a table outside the school building. The presiding officer would then mark the person's name and registration number in a docket book. (Curiously, although registration cards had a voter's thumbprint, registration number, and polling station marked on them, they did not have the voter's name.) The agent could then tear off a single ballot from a pile, stamp it on the back with a FEDECO rubber stamp, hand it with a FEDECO envelope to the voter, and explain what the voter was to do with it.

The ballots for each of the five elections were identical. No names of candidates ever appeared, nor were the parties' names ever spelled out. Rather, the parties' symbols and initials were printed in square-inch boxes, presented vertically and in alphabetical order. The Great Nigerian People's Party's symbol was a large tree, shading a cow, a chicken, and an oil well. A pair of hands holding a globe of Nigeria represented the Nigeria Advance Party, while a house surrounded by corn announced the National Party of Nigeria. The National People's Party showed a couple with their two children, with the People's Redemption Party picturing a simple key. A lighted torch superimposed on the shape of Nigeria was the sign of the Unity Party of Nigeria. Beside each

Sample Ballot, 1983 Elections

box with a party symbol was an empty box of the same dimension.

Each voter was instructed to enter the schoolroom alone, with his ballot and envelope. Behind an aluminum screen was an inkpad placed on a table. He was to place his thumb on the pad, then put his print in the box next to his preferred party's symbol. Before leaving the room, he was supposed to place the ballot in the envelope. Once outside, he was to place the envelope in the heavy, metal ballot box, marked "FEDECO," that stood on a table in full view of everyone. Before leaving the polling station, the voter had his finger daubed, between the nail and the flesh, with "indelible" red ink. This was supposed to prevent people from voting more than once. (See the Sample Ballot, 1983 Elections.)

Although outside accounts of the voting reported it as a fairly simple, straightforward procedure, the events in Yardaji demonstrated that at least for people in the bush, *zabe* (voting) could be a rather bewildering, incomprehensible experience.

Women in particular (probably since they have even less familiarity with manipulating paper and related paraphernalia than do men) evinced great difficulty in following these instructions. Frequently, a voter would exit from the classroom without having placed the ballot in the envelope. This sometimes revealed that the voter had neglected to make any mark on the ballot. (Apparently, many thought that marking the thumb with ink constituted the principal gesture.) For some, placing a slip of paper in an envelope was beyond their manual dexterity. Others lacked the eye-hand coordination necessary to slip the envelope into the slit of the ballot box. One old man wandered off from the polling station, unnoticed, with his ballot and envelope in hand.[4] Another, thinking that the red ink smeared on his fingernail by the polling agent was actually medicine, requested that his other hand be "treated" as well! One woman, looking lost and puzzled, blurted out her excuse— or defense— for having endured this electoral "ordeal": "Allah *ya kawomu* !" ("*God* brought us here!")

Nevertheless, the turnout, even for the first election day, was quite respectable. As mentioned earlier, Fulanis traveled substantial distances, on foot and in the powerful daytime heat, to get to the Yardaji polls. Very old people participated. Crippled and deformed villagers limped over. The half-blind and totally blind voted. Even an apparent mental retard (although his principal disorder might have been deafness) exercised his civic rights, making rather uncommon sounds and gestures as he did so. In short, even with minimal understanding of politics, candidates, parties, or platforms, and in the absence of any coercion to do so, people from even the most peripheral areas elected to vote—because in some sense they felt it was *right* to do so. This, perhaps, was the most important "election" of all.

The greatest "drama" of that first election day in Yardaji occurred around 10:00 A.M., when *Mai-gari* Alhaji Haruna, the chief of Yardaji, arrived at the "eastern school" to vote. In general, the chief rarely left his outer courtyard to move about the village; he was virtually never seen in any crowd of people. (Villagers did, however, continuously come to greet, consult, and arbitrate through him outside his abode.) For the chief to appear at the schoolhouse, among the group of voting *talakawa*, was perhaps the most "leveling" occurrence that he might ever experience.

The chief, of course, was not expected to wait in line, and was given a chair on the porch of the schoolhouse. Voting went on as usual, although many villagers respectfully moved back to accord him space, while others extended the customary greeting by bowing. Nevertheless, with the chief sitting on the porch and the villagers standing in line, a most exceptional altitudinal relationship was established: perhaps for the first time, the chief was literally on the same "level" as his people. (Hausa custom obliges social inferiors to stoop or bow in the presence of their superiors. For a villager to remain standing in front of his chief would ordinarily be an act of disrespect, arrogance, or presumption.) Even if in terms of spatial geography alone, modern participatory

In Northern Nigeria, women were extended the vote in 1979.

democracy had, at least for a fleeting moment, made its "equal-izing" statement in far-off Yardaji.

When the time had come, and the chief had voted, the de-nouement of the electoral drama in Yardaji occurred: would even *Mai-gari* have to have his finger smeared with indelible red ink? As *Mai-gari* emerged from the voting booth, a polling agent pre-pared his brush with ink. Seeing this, Alhaji Kosso, the chief's courtier, demurred, claiming that daubing was unnecessary for the chief. The agent insisted, "It's the same for 'Them' as well." (*Su ma, duk daya ne.*) The chief diplomatically resolved the stand-off by drawing away his hand with a good-natured laugh, while uttering an incontrovertible "No!" The confrontation may have been minor, but it serves as illustration of the wedge that the electoral process—even on a microcosmic, village level—invaria-bly creates between secular and traditional sources, modes, and norms of authority in the dual polity of Nigerian Hausaland.

Throughout the day, the Yardaji polling stations were peri-odically visited by FEDECO officials from Daura. The two police-men, never apart, also periodically shuttled between the two schools. Apart from these outside elements, voting in Yardaji was basically an intravillage affair; overt "penetration" from the politi-cal center was relatively minor. Many observers[5] of the 1983 elec-tions concur that, while widespread "irregularities" characterized the later elections (i.e., for national and state representatives), the presidential election was relatively "free and fair." In fact, they may indeed have been "free" (in the sense that all parties were "free" to garner votes in whatever way they saw fit), but that they were "fair" remains even less open to such definitionally liberal gamesmanship.

Even in Yardaji, "irregularities" in that August 6 contest ex-isted. A minor example: late in the afternoon of that first presi-dential election, an NPN "activist" asked some women if they had voted. Stating that they didn't have any registration cards—which legally should have ruled out their participation—the man promised to supply them with necessary cards. Without mention as to its significance, he instructed: "They'll give you a paper with six pictures. When you see corn and a house, put your finger-print." He never explained that "corn and a house" meant "NPN" or "Shagari." Although perhaps isolated and insignificant, the ex-ample presages later and more serious "irregularities."

After 6:00 P.M., with dusk approaching,[6] the ballot boxes were opened (with two separate keys), and the counting began. Only now would the voters' choice be counted—and the counters' minds confused.

As the ballots were stacked according to party, it soon became apparent that many voters never really understood what was expected of them behind the aluminum screen, with the ink-pad. Ballots had thumbprints, or smudges, in the most unlikely places. Some had prints in or over several or all of the boxes, while some had no prints at all. Some had prints *on* the party's symbol, and not in the designated box next to it. Some ballots called for highly subjective decisions—e.g., a clean, dark print in a single box, but with a (inadvertent?) smudge in the box of some other party (with varying degrees of darkness between the two). Some, having made a clear choice in applying thumb to box, had hopelessly smudged the ballot as they fumbled to place it in the envelope. At least one presiding officer contemptuously referred to these *damaji* (invalid votes) as "woman's work."

A strict interpretation of the electoral laws might easily have disqualified the overwhelming majority of the ballots. Polling agents agreed to make a separate pile of the *damaji*, and to allocate, by mutual consensus, the less flagrant of them to the various parties. Even then, in at least one of the stations, the final number of *damaji* (even after the "grey" ones had been reconsidered and distributed) equaled or exceeded the number of votes for any one of the parties. Indeed, even if there arose some mutually agreed-upon standard for evaluating *damaji* at each individual polling station, there was certainly no uniform policy in force from one station to the next. Since Nigerian electoral statistics do not reflect "invalid votes" (as do, for instance, French electoral statistics), it is impossible to know the true extent of this hitherto neglected variable in the Nigerian elections.

Once the ballots were counted, the results were noted on official tally sheets, one for each polling station. These tally sheets were signed by each of the parties' polling agents and the presiding officers officiating at each station. The tally sheets were then sent off, individually, to the district tally center in Rogogo, together with the used and unused ballots, the ballot box, stamps, and all voting paraphernalia. Successive levels of tally centers accumulated the results from polling stations throughout their jurisdictions, passing them up the chain of command, until FEDECO in Lagos had its "grand tally."

CHAPTER ELEVEN

The Results

THE PRESIDENTIAL RESULTS

Inasmuch as the Nigerian government never released an official breakdown of the electoral results by polling station, it is difficult to know if the figures recorded in Yardaji, for instance, corresponded with those ultimately registered for that constituency by FEDECO. More comprehensive accounts of the elections throughout all of Nigeria mitigate against any faith in the accuracy of the final results as released by FEDECO (although it has been rationalized—by the U.S. embassy in Lagos, among others—that Shagari "would have won anyway," even *if* the elections had been completely honest).[1] To offer the official results without providing this *caveat* would be to lend a spurious credibility to them. Moreover, as we have seen in Yardaji, even in the absence of direct tampering or improper intentions, a good many of the ballots necessitated a somewhat arbitrary judgment by polling agents to determine whom the voter *meant* to vote for. That is, even in the absence of conscious impropriety, the fact that a good proportion of voters simply might not have known what they were doing casts further clouds over the legitimacy of the elections. (This assumes, admittedly, that the experience of Yardaji was not unique.) By way of example, it is hardly likely that any of the thirty-two persons whose ballots were allocated to NAP— the only party in Yardaji with absolutely no representation or profile— had any intention of voting for Tunji Braithwaite.

Nevertheless, having cast sufficient doubt as to the reliability of the electoral results (and especially the correlation between political intent and voting act), the figures remain, and demand scrutiny. In no democratic system can the voter's mind, even as he casts a ballot, be read; it is, rather, the final output that must be scrutinized.

Since polling stations results were sent directly to the tally center, without even being compiled in the village itself, no single, cumulative record for Yardaji as a whole was kept by any official. However, a compilation of the records kept by polling agents from the nine stations in the village render the cumulative results for Yardaji. These are contrasted, where appropriate, with district, national, and statewide results, to provide a comparative perspective. Once again, the accuracy of the results is in inverse proportion to scale; i.e., the figures collected in Yardaji may be regarded as more reliable than those issued nationally by FEDECO. (See Table 11.1.)

There are five striking differences between the results in Yardaji compared with the totality of Nigeria. One is the much more balanced distribution in the village than in the country as a whole. Except for UPN, each opposition party scored significantly better in Yardaji than throughout Nigeria. Given Nigeria's extreme ethnic, linguistic, and religious heterogeneity, and Yardaji's no less extreme homogeneity along these same lines, it is highly significant that the village exhibited greater party balance than Nigeria as a whole.

Second, the fact that Shehu Shagari, although gaining a plurality in the village, nevertheless scored almost twelve percentage points *below* the national average is remarkable. Where else would one— reasoning as an "ethnic arithmetician"— expect a Shagari landslide, if not in a small, traditional, rural, Northern, Muslim, and Hausa community? Yet Shagari was far from receiving villagewide unanimity. A third factor is the highly respectable showing, in Hausa Yardaji, of Nnamdi Azikiwe, the Igbo presidential candidate of the Nigerian People's Party. It is true that, in the North, the NPP had the backing of some notable Hausa personalities (such as Governor Abubakar Rimi of Kano state) and therefore was not perceived in Yardaji as an essentially Igbo party. But it is this very fact that testifies to the ethnic secularization of the parties (a far cry from the First Republic, when the NCNC, NPC, and Action Group parties could legitimately be labeled "Eastern," "Northern," and "Western" in expression and constituency). The Yardaji Azikiwe vote was perhaps most impor-

Table 11.1   Results of 1983 Presidential Elections

Candidate	Party	Yardaji Village		Zango District		Kaduna State		Nigeria Republic	
		Votes	%	Votes	%	Votes	%	Votes	%
Shagari	NPN	356	(35.6)	5,804	(34.5)	1,266,894	(59.3)	12,081,471	(47.5)
Yusuf	PRP	239	(23.9)	5,345	(31.7)	300,476	(14.0)	968,974	(03.8)
Waziri	GNPP	92	(09.2)	1,549	(09.2)	80,862	(03.8)	643,805	(02.5)
Awolowo	UPN	46	(04.6)	759	(04.5)	225,878	(10.6)	7,907,209	(31.2)
Azikiwe	NPP	234	(23.4)	2,574	(15.3)	225,919	(10.6)	3,557,113	(14.0)
Braithwaite	NAP	32	(03.2)	795	(04.7)	37,369	(01.8)	271,524	(01.0)
Total		999		16,826		2,137,398		25,430,096	

Sources: Africa Research Bulletin (August 1–31, 1983): 6937;
West Africa (August 15, 1983): 1866; Author's field notes.

Table 11.2   Results of 1983 Gubernatorial Elections

Candidate (in Kaduna State)	Party	Yardaji		Kaduna State		Nigeria	
		Votes	%	Votes	%	Votes	%
Lawal Kaita	NPN	248	(23.1)	2,144,069	(64.9)	20,298,167	(57.5)
Musa Musawa	PRP	512	(47.7)	480,169	(14.7)	1,390,217	(03.9)
Sabiu Nuhu	GNPP	57	(05.3)	71,401	(02.2)	573,366	(01.6)
Muhammed Jumare	UPN	21	(02.0)	135,911	(04.2)	8,290,618	(23.5)
Yinusa Yusuf	NPP	222	(20.1)	420,526	(12.9)	4,523,299	(12.8)
Baba Danladi	NAP	14	(01.3)	71,401	(02.2)	573,366	(01.6)
Total		1,074		3,255,194[a]		35,280,300[b]	

[a]This is the figure as published. From subtotals provided, total should be 3,323,477.

[b]This is the figure as published. From subtotals provided, total should be 35,649,033.

Sources: West Africa (August 22, 1983): 1925; Author's field notes.

Table 11.3 Results of 1983 Senatorial Elections

Candidate (in Daura-Kenkiya-Mani Constituency)	Party	Yardaji Votes	%	Kaduna State Seats	%	Nigeria Seats	%
Abdou Mashi	NPN	546	(24.2)	5	(100)	55	(64.7)
Alhaji Tijani	PRP	1,457	(64.8)	0	(0)	5	(05.9)
Alhaji Lawal	GNPP	30	(01.3)	0	(0)	1	(01.1)
Abdullahi Fako	UPN	45	(02.0)	0	(0)	12	(14.1)
Alhaji Audu	NPP	137	(06.0)	0	(0)	12	(14.1)
No Candidate	NAP	33	(01.4)	0	(0)	0	(00.0)
Total		2,248		5		85[a]	

[a] Does not include Oyo and Ondo states (10 seats).

Sources: Africa Research Bulletin (August 1-31, 1983): 6940; Author's field notes.

Table 11.4 Results of 1983 House of Representatives Elections

Candidate (in Zango-Baure Constituency)	Party	Yardaji Votes	%	Kaduna State Seats	%	Nigeria Seats	%
Manzo Abubakar	NPN	580	(24.5)	33	(100)	264	(100.0)
Sani Danda	PRP	139	(05.8)	0	(0)	41	(10.6)
Awali Issaka	GNPP	115	(04.8)	0	(0)	0	(00.0)
Ahmadu Ciccila	UPN	25	(01.0)	0	(0)	33	(08.5)
Alhaji Sani	NPP	1,490	(62.9)	0	(0)	48	(12.4)
No Candidate	NAP	17	(00.7)	0	(0)	0	(00.0)
Total		2,366		33		386a	

[a] Does not include Oyo and Ondo states (64 seats)

Sources: West Africa (September 12, 1983): 2150; Author's field notes.

Table 11.5 Results of 1983 State Assembly Elections

Candidate (in Zango Local Government)	Party	Yardaji (Village Station Records) Votes	%	Yardaji (Tally Center Records) Votes	%	Zango Local Government Votes	%
Galadima Ya'u	NPN	1,572	(54.1)	1,970	(52.1)	22,016	(45.5)
Malam Shefiou	PRP	345	(11.8)	16	(0.4)	1,750	(03.6)
Na'awa Usman	GNPP	285	(09.8)	272	(07.2)	4,596	(09.5)
Malam Mudaha	UPN	22	(00.7)	1,135	(30.0)	10,877	(22.5)
Badamasi Lawal	NPP	664	(22.8)	370	(09.8)	8,556	(17.7)
No Candidate	NAP	16	(00.5)	15	(00.4)	542	(01.1)
Total		2,904		3,778		48,337	

Source: Author's field notes.

tant, then, for what it demonstrated in a negative sense: that Hausa villagers will not vote against a presidential contender merely because he is an Igbo.

Fourth, note the People Redemption Party's high score in Yardaji, compared nationally, coming in second as opposed to fourth (24 percent *vs.* 4 percent). This is not surprising, given the PRP's long-standing goal to mobilize the underprivileged Northern peasantry against the so-called Hausa-Fulani aristocracy—a somewhat parochial (in national terms) appeal. The PRP suffered a blow by the untimely death of its founder and leader, Mallam Aminu Kano, just four months before the elections. Hassan Yusuf, the new PRP candidate, was less known than Kano had been, and probably could not garner the same support as his predecessor. Even so, Yusuf's PRP posed a serious challenge to Shagari's NPN in Yardaji, a challenge that might have been even a greater threat had not Aminu Kano died so precipitously.

The low UPN vote in Yardaji demands a final comment, for it too is at striking variance with the national average. Of course, due to historical and ethnic factors, nowhere in the North could UPN prevail. But other factors mattered too. Although represented by party leaders in Zango and Yardaji, UPN simply did not demonstrate the organizational and financial strength of the other parties. (The fact that the "Awo" vehicle was a Volkswagen Beetle, as opposed to a Nissan minibus, was a visible, and constant, reminder of this.) Moreover, as ethnic affiliation surveys conducted throughout the village show, Yorubas were even more highly regarded than Igbos (although Awolowo's ethnic background was certainly no help to local UPN efforts). Ethnic considerations thus should be relativized by perhaps more relevant, if prosaic, factors, such as the low level of campaign investment and lack of effective grassroots party organization in the village.

In short, the fact that each of the Nigerian parties (with the exception of NAP) was represented in Yardaji by native village party representatives translated into an overall, relatively balanced vote distribution in the August 6 polls. Considering his ethnicity and incumbency, Shagari, while the principal vote-getter, actually performed rather modestly. Since the official (i.e., national) figures cannot be taken at their face value, moreover, the Yardaji numbers can serve two broader functions: they may provide even further evidence to question the legitimacy of the officially reported results (i.e., if Shagari received only 35 percent in a 100 percent Northern, Muslim, Hausa village, how could he have actually scored 48 percent nationwide?), and may be used to demonstrate, however belatedly, the success of electoral ethnic secularization under the Second Republic.

THE GUBERNATORIAL RESULTS

With the gubernatorial elections on August 13, the nationwide slide toward NPN electoral domination began to take shape. So did the dubiousness of the reported results.

In one week, the number of "voters" jumped ten million, to 35,280,300. NPN swept thirteen out of nineteen governorships, giving rise to anti-NPN rioting and deaths in a number of states (especially in Oyo and Ondo). In Kaduna state, NPN candidate Lawal Kaita won by a landslide (65 percent). In placid Yardaji, however, results compiled from the polling stations themselves showed that, once again, the village voted against the grain of the nation (at least as officially reported). (See Table 11.2.)

As the table reveals, PRP candidate Musawa took Yardaji by storm, with 12 percent more votes than even President Shagari had gotten a week earlier. NPN candidate Kaita, despite his alleged landslide, had 40 percent fewer votes in Yardaji than the statewide average.

Even in Yardaji, rumors began circulating that PRP candidate Musa Musawa had actually won in Kaduna state, but was given "millions of naira" to accept his defeat; or, he was to be given a cushy, high-paying job in the new administration. In any event, with growing news of fraud and rigging throughout the state and nation, Yardaji-ites might be excused for beginning to wonder if they too were participating in the elections in "the Nigerian way."

Some villagers claimed that it was impossible for electoral *murdiya* ("twisting") to go on in Yardaji itself, for the people there lacked sufficient *ilmi* (education, learning) to do so.[2] Be that as it may, a new attitude in the village could be inferred— that *not* to engage in electoral *wayo* (cunning) was more a reflection of a backward, "hick" mentality than anything else. 'The entire country is doing it— what is the matter with Yardaji? Are we not as sharp as others, as city folk? All of Nigeria is playing the game by different rules than Yardaji. What's the matter with us?'

SENATORIAL AND REPRESENTATIVE RESULTS

I was unfortunately unable to be in Yardaji to monitor the two following elections, for Senate and House of Representatives. It therefore cannot be said what the village results, as counted at the polling stations, actually were. However, party leaders in Zango kept records of the figures as they were reported to the district tally center. Note the rather untenable inflation in terms of recorded votes, which rise from approximately one thousand (in the presidential and gubernatorial rounds) to around twenty-three hundred for the Senate and House elections. (See Tables 11.3. and 11.4.)

Even in Yardaji, the relatively balanced distribution of recorded votes of the presidential and (to a lesser extent) gubernatorial elections falls apart. Alhaji Tijani, senatorial candidate of the PRP, won by a lopsided margin in Yardaji, as did Alhaji Sani, House representative candidate of the NPP. Again, the source of the data makes it impossible to say if any irregularities took place at the level of the Yardaji polling stations, or higher up the tally hierarchy. It is relevant to note, however, that of the two victors in Yardaji, Alhaji Tijani hailed from nearby Zango, and Alhaji Sani was himself a native village son.

STATE ASSEMBLY RESULTS

If there remained an illusion about Yardaji's pristine, virtuous, and therefore unique conduct throughout the entire electoral season, these were shattered at the last of the five contests— the vote for state assemblyman. If "extenuating circumstances" may be invoked, they would include the fact that one of the candidates for the position was not only a proverbial native village son but the actual, biological offspring of the village chief.[3] Also, by this time in the elections, it was known that "devices" were used throughout the entire nation to ensure that "favored" candidates were, in fact, "elected."

Around mid-morning, Alhaji Galadima, the favored candidate arrived— with the local FEDECO official— to determine the participation rate. Told that the turnout was theretofore slow, he instructed a town-crier to make a "proclamation" throughout the village, to encourage people to vote. For his effort, the candidate gave the villager a crisp, new naira note.[4]

This vignette admirably portrays the problem in applying conventional, western norms concerning electoral conduct and behavior— which are nevertheless western-derived phenomena— in places like Yardaji. For a U.S. candidate to appear at the voting booths and then publicly (or even privately) give people money to "drum up participation" would certainly transgress a host of ethical and legal codes. Should the Yardaji candidate be similarly judged? To encourage electoral participation in and of itself is not improper— party organizers do this throughout election day in the United States as well. It is the transfer of money that probably evokes the greatest quandary. But that a crier be asked to circulate throughout a village without some sort of monetary recompense— *not* as payment but as appreciation or acknowledgment of his efforts *(kokari)*— would itself violate Hausa norms of conduct and propriety, particularly that of *mutunci* (self-respect).

Throughout the day, the polling stations conducted normal business, to facilitate the actual ballot-casting by villagers and Fulanis alike. By 5:00 P.M., however, one hour before the designated closing time, at least two stations were turning away potential voters and already "tallying" the votes.

In at least one station, this consisted of peeling off prestamped ballots[5] (i.e., those with fingerprints already marked in boxes) from a full wad and placing them with the legitimate ones. Some arithmetic calculation was done so that the results recorded on the official tally sheets would correspond to the total number of ballots (i.e., premarked plus properly marked ones). All election materials were then neatly put away in the ballot box, according to regulation, including FEDECO pamphlet Number 6: "Order and Electoral Offenses."

Although village turnout in this last election appeared the lowest, the results— as indicated on the polling station tally sheets— reflected an almost tripling in actual votes cast. But even further inflation at the level of the tally center apparently went on. A comparison of the results reported by the village polling stations with those registered for Yardaji by polling agents in Zango reveals a further 30 percent jump in the number of votes actually recorded. (See Table 11.5.)

That night, when word arrived that Alhaji Galadima had in fact won the election, Yardaji was ecstatic. The village cry of success— *"Gari, ya yi kyau"* ("All is well for the town!")— went out, and *Mai-gari* not only left his inner chambers but, in an unusual act, joined his confidants, sitting on mats on the ground. Official celebrations were held in the village a few nights later, when Al-haji Galadima was present. Amidst dancing and drumming, the victor handed out many crisp naira notes as villagers came to offer their congratulations and respect (*gaisuwa*), and women made their famous piercing, shrill cries of victory, success, and happiness.

When pressed about the elections, an informant finally ad-mitted that the village had engaged in some stratagem, or wile (*dubara*), to get a "son of the town" elected. (This included giving three or four naira to the onlooking policemen to "drink por-ridge.") Not to have done their utmost would not only have been unworthy, vis-à-vis their "native son," but self-defeating for the community as a whole: if their own Galadima were not elected, who else would ever bother to bring the village electricity, run-ning water, and a paved road?

Dubara was facilitated by the fact that, since only NPN poll-ing agents had until that point been paid, agents of the other par-ties no longer bothered to supervise the voting. (This "payment" was seen as compensation for services performed.) The fact that other parties didn't bother to pay their workers was regarded as further proof of these parties' undependability.

The *dubara* that Yardaji-ites engaged in, however inexcusable in an absolute sense, had been made somewhat inevitable by the path that "democracy" had taken throughout, and even before, the electoral period. *Dubara* was a euphemism for conduct that they knew was in some sense improper but nevertheless prac-ticed throughout the nation. Even Yardaji could not remain forever isolated from the reality of Nigerian politics.

The village's ultimate attitude to electoral politics might best be described as "reluctant pragmatism." Yardaji "joined" the elec-toral system because it had no choice, and despite the conflict that pitted Hausa values and social structure against the egali-tarian ethos of modern democratic politics. It was forced to cope, even as the new system, however discredited in its unfolding manifestations, was gnawing away at the old.

CHAPTER TWELVE

The Coup

On January 1, 1984, Nigeria's Second Republic came to a sudden death. The night before, on New Year's Eve, the Nigerian military high command, in response to a rapidly deteriorating economic crisis, and desirous of forestalling a takeover by junior (and, presumably, more radical) officers, toppled the civilian government of Shehu Shagari in a virtually bloodless coup d'état. (Only one fatality, that of Brig. Ibrahim Bako, who resisted the president's arrest, was ever reported.) Once again, but more unexpectedly, Yardaji was forced to confront the reality of Nigerian "politics." [1]

Information concerning the most recent developments arrived in the village in less than direct fashion. Some villagers were tipped off early in the morning of New Year's Day, when Radio Kaduna began playing western classical orchestral music. (This is popularly believed to be martial music, and to presage important military announcements.) Then, a prerecorded proclamation by Brig. Sani Abacha was broadcast, announcing the formation of a new "Federal Military Government of the Republic of Nigeria," the dismissal of all elected officials, the suspension of most of the constitution, and the closing of the country's airports, seaports, land borders, and international telecommunications systems. The recording was repeated every twenty minutes or so, between the telltale "military" interludes.

Unfortunately, for all but a handful of village residents, the coup announcement itself was incomprehensible, for it was in *Turanci* (English). So was the radio announcement of the following day, when the new head of state addressed the nation for the first time. In fact, a full forty-eight hours were to pass before Nigerian radio stations announced news of the coup in Hausa, the only vernacular that most Northern Nigerians can understand. Until then, Yardaji-ites had to be satisfied first with the translations that the few English-speakers residing in the village (basically the schoolteachers and author) could provide, and then with the Hausa language shortwave programs of the BBC, Voice of America, and the Voice of Germany.

When informed of the coup, the typical reaction expressed a twofold concern. The first dealt with the physical welfare of the (now deposed) president. Given the rather bloody precedents in Nigerian regime takeovers and coup attempts (e.g., the assassinations of popular Northern-born leaders, Prime Minister Tafawa Balewa, Premier Ahmadu Bello, and Gen. Murtala Mohammed), there was great relief when it was learned that Shehu Shagari's life had been spared. According to *Mai-gari*, "At least, it could have been worse. As long as they didn't kill the President. . . ."

The second preoccupation dealt with the economic implications of having a military regime. As one villager put it, "May God bring us good fortune, and may the price of Omo come down!" (Several days later, this faith in the ability of the military to set things right again with the economy was reinforced in verse and song, on the airwaves. *Na ga soji*, crooned one balladeer, *na ga abinci* : "I was a soldier, [and then] I saw food."

Immediate comment on the coup often took the form of proverb and parable. "When the dogs gather round, and a hyena comes and howls, what do they do? Why, run!" By this account, the politicians are the "dogs," the soldier the "hyena." When "dogs" gather about, make a racket and play, is it not necessary for someone to come and scatter them? The notion of play— *wasa*— was consistently used to characterize the "white-capped" regime. Democracy and civilian politics were thus described as playthings, toys, or jokes, certainly not anything to be taken seriously— not as seriously, at least, as rule by the *bindiga* : the gun.

The democratic fallacy of not paying proper attention to the legitimate hierarchy of power and rank (*iko* and *daraja*) was invoked in the rhetorical, if chauvinistic, query: "Do you put a woman in front of her husband?" A younger villager broached this subject more directly: "Everybody [under the civilian regime] had the freedom to insult. I am a nobody. But if I had a grudge against someone, even someone 'big,' I could have gone to the

Radio Station and 'insult' that person publicly. Now, no one will dare criticize the people at the top. Fear!"

The same idea was expressed by an older villager, in more eloquent terms: "Respect will now return to society. . . . In the past, whether someone was a man of wealth or royalty, he would be addressed in any manner whatsoever. Now, the rulers will be treated with respect. No more insulting of leaders. *Babu zage*."

The disorder, the chaos that had passed as government was now over. Hausa imagery conveyed this in spatial terms: "Before, there was wandering [in the body politic]; now, government is in one place." Other sentiments expressed were: "Now there will be greater justice—no one will get away with crimes because of his money." "Only the soldier really knows how to rule." "What business is it of ours? We're only peasants. [*Ina ruwamu? Muna talakawa.*]" "The leaders were ignoring the plight of the common man—they had excrement in their ears" (i.e., they didn't hear what was going on with the people).

One special Yardaji-ite—special, because he worked during the week in Kano as the clerk/accountant in a large department store—was able to discuss the failure of Nigeria's experiment in a comparative light: "We just weren't capable of a democratic system like yours. We're not the same. With you, everyone has learning. Here, there is too much illiteracy. Even the elected officials are illiterate."

As an example, he recalled the time that a state representative came to his company to pick up a government car loan, but was unable to sign even his name. He could only put his fingerprint on the document.

It would be misleading, however, to give the impression that all villagers were uniformly, and unqualifiably, happy about the military takeover. One elderly man, citing the restriction in trade that military government in nearby Niger engendered, noted that "not a single goat had arrived from 'France'" since the coup was announced. A more underlying concern, at least before the composition of the military's ruling council was announced, also invited caution for some: "The leaders we had were our own stock—but what about the new ones?" And one advanced *alhaji*, while not defending Shagari directly, did try to mitigate the former leader's shortcomings by invoking a recognized Hausa standard of propriety and right conduct: *kunya. Kunya* is usually translated as "shame," but it also more fully encompasses the sense of responsibility one has not to demean one's reputation, manhood, or respect—be it of oneself or someone else. Thus, Alhaji

Lassan reasoned, "His ministers were corrupt, all right, but Shagari didn't do anything about it— because of *kumya*. *That* was his
wrong." Put slightly differently, even at the highest levels of
government, Hausa social custom and duty were in conflict with
the executive imperatives of managing a modern, bureaucratic
state. In the end, corruption won out over *kumya*.

Yardaji's involvement in the political developments of the
country at large was not confined to social commentary. By virtue
of the village's geographical position— walking distance from the
international boundary with Niger Republic— Yardaji was henceforth to be "visited" frequently by uniformed agents of the customs, immigration, and police forces, who were to patrol the
border areas for ex-politicians attempting to flee the country.
(One would-be refugee *was* caught in the nearby village of Garke;
he reportedly was trying to smuggle out "two or three vehicles,
several women, and much property." When he saw the border
patrol, he fled on foot, leaving the women and vehicle behind.)

The role of these authorities was not confined to their attempts to seal the borders. There was a local impact as well. Immediately after the coup, a nationwide curfew had been
proclaimed in Lagos by the country's new leaders. For the cities
and towns, there was perhaps understandable justification for
this measure. Imposing a curfew in remote villages, on the other
hand, bordered on the absurd. The curfew forbade people from
leaving their homes at night; in the villages, after dark, men con-
gregate just in *front* of their homes, on mats, to chat, and will
often sleep there as well.

A curfew is a curfew, however, and the patrolling, uniformed
immigration officers considered it their duty to enforce it, even
in the bush. Discovering some villagers who were sitting and
chatting outside, on the ground, they fell upon them with whips,
ordering them inside their compounds. The famous "War Against
Indiscipline"— that austere policy that came to typify the immediate post-Shagari era— was already being waged in far off
Yardaji, even before the campaign had been declared. The irony
is that these zealous paramilitary authorities were already ex-
ceeding their duty: at the time of the Yardaji whippings, the radio
had already announced that the curfew had been lifted.

Despite the seriousness of the country's political situation,
and the ominous foreshadowing (by way of the curfew whippings)
of what military rule could mean for ordinary citizens, Yardaji-

ites also reacted to the events with characteristic humor. One manifestation was the new kind of salutation with which a visitor might be greeted while passing in the street. Stopping short, in mid-stride, a villager would stomp his right foot firmly on the ground and raise his open-palmed hand to his forehead in mock salute, smiling broadly. *Saboda mulkin soji*, it would be said: "On account of the military government."

The most revealing attitudes toward the coup d'état, nevertheless, were not expressed until the day following the coup, when the identity of the new head of state was announced. Until then, most of Yardaji did join in like measure with the rest of Nigeria, in welcoming the return of the military, the sweeping away of civilian government, and the complete banishing of *siyasa*. Politics had, from the village vantage, proven itself to be not only culturally undesirable but positively unworkable. Even those who *had* actively participated in the campaign and elections of the previous summer were gratified; their earlier electoral participation could now be dismissed as an activity they were obliged to undertake by default, but one which they were now just as happy to do without. *Talakawa* expressed relief that henceforth they, mere village folk and peasants, were relieved of the responsibility to engage in elections, politics, "democracy"— processes that they had never quite mastered or controlled in the first place, but which they had been pressured to participate in nevertheless.

On January 2, 1984, Yardaji's particular pleasure was all the more enhanced when the community learned that the new Nigerian head of state was none other than Maj. Gen. Muhammadu Buhari, a native of nearby Daura, and a man known personally to people throughout the village. The town crier announced the news ecstatically with the formula, "It's a New World!" and even the chief joked good-humoredly, "*Mu ne sarauta yanzu*"— "Now, *we* are the rulers of Nigeria!" (For was Yardaji not an integral part of Daura emirate, and "Daura" now in charge in Lagos?) Not only did Nigeria have a new ruler, celebrated the people in Yardaji, but this time he was truly one of "theirs."

Postscript

Three and a half years later, when I returned to Yardaji in the summer of 1986, Nigeria was still under *mulkin soja*. The initial honeymoon with the military had long since ended, and Buhari himself, deposed in August of 1985, was now in detention. The "strong hand" of the military that had been welcomed throughout the country initially was now perceived as repressive, and Buhari's much-heralded "War Against Indiscipline" ignominiously forgotten. Another, supposedly more liberal, faction of the military was now in power, headed by Maj. Gen. Ibrahim Babangida. Talk of an eventual return to democracy could already be heard (at least amongst the country's elite and intelligentsia), and even a timetable— 1990— tentatively proffered as due date for the Third Republic.[1]

As might be expected, however, the prospect of a return to the *farin fula* was not generating much enthusiasm in Yardaji. Buhari's own deposition had not gone over very well, either. For sure, the people of Yardaji had felt the whip (literally as well as figuratively) of the Buhari era; unlawful crossing of the border (not reopened until March of 1986) was severely dealt with, and the government itself was likened to that of next-door Niger (never a favorable comparison, as far as Yardaji-ites are concerned). But, it was felt, discipline had returned to Nigeria, crime throughout the country was down, and— perhaps most important— so were prices. Babangida's rule coincided, at least in the villagers' eyes, with the return of inflation, as well as with other negative aspects of pre-Buhari Nigeria (e.g., open and widespread bribery).

Of course, it would be naive to preclude the more obvious explanation for Yardaji's disillusionment with the present turn of Nigerian politics: their "own" son of Daura had been ousted from power, and any hope of dramatic improvement through chiefly largesse swept away as well. Once again, the transience of "modern" leadership—which may rightfully be viewed to encompass military rulers as well as civilian ones—was demonstrated. And once again, there was little in this transience of state that was seen to bode well for the people.

The "real" chiefs, of course, still hold seat, and believe at least as much as the *talakawa* that *they* hold the key to legitimacy. An interview with the emir of Daura, paraphrased below, points this out:

> People who espouse "democracy" are saying it just for the sake of their mouths—but not as a matter of truth. Every army regime discovers that it cannot dispense with the traditional rulers, because they need them. A true army man cares about competence—wherever it may be. Therefore, the military turns, naturally and inevitably, to the traditional leaders. Unfortunately, the "elite" (the graduates, those who presumably have *ilmi*, but actually are not helping the country) prevent the army from going to and using the traditional leaders, who are the best administrators for the country.
>
> Of course there will be corruption in politics. If a man spends a million naira to be elected, won't he try to get it back once he's in office? And will he be able to dispense true justice, when he is beholden to the people for election? . . . In the past, in addition to the popularity and honesty of the traditional leader, it was important that he be independently wealthy—just so that he *not* have to be beholden to the people of his community.[2]

In somewhat different terms, a farmer back in Yardaji expressed the same belief concerning the (inevitable) link between politicians and money: "When [your wife] wants her cat to come to her, what does she do? She gives it some milk. Or if you wish to befriend a dog, don't you give it a piece of meat? So it is in politics. . . ."

Inevitably, some new system of electoral politics will be introduced in Nigeria. Perhaps, and for the first time since the *mulkin Turawa*, it will be a truly indigenous, and homespun, African system. This modest study of elections in Yardaji cannot hope to provide the model for a future Nigerian government; however, if it convinces the reader that, in this African land now called "Nigeria," a radically different (and yet familiar!) approach to politics is in order, then it will have more than adequately fulfilled its mission. As an example of possible future inquiry, consider the prevailing fetishism for *partisan* politics.

When the Westminster parliamentary system was introduced for the First Republic, it was taken for granted that political parties would be the keystone to Nigerian political competition. When the Constitutional Drafting Committee met to design the Second Republic, it again embraced the notion of political organization based on competitive parties. Rarely were the ideological differences between the parties so clear-cut as to be truly meaningful; certainly, party platform meant little to the ordinary voter. Precious little assures that political parties in the future will be any more conducive to either ideological awareness or systemic efficiency in Nigeria. The opportunity to rethink this, as well as all the other, supposed *sine qua nons* of "modern" political systems is presenting itself. May the opportunity be seized.

Political legitimacy cannot be created overnight; the Nigerian experience indicates that even a quarter of a century may be insufficient time to generate a widely accepted basis for rulership and governance. Certainly, political parties *per se* are not the cause of political failure in Nigeria. They are, however, components of manifestly unworkable experiments that have taken their lead from far, far away. Legitimacy, it should not be forgotten, begins at home. Where legitimacy derives from tradition, tradition itself must be given an honest, fair, and unprejudged appraisal.

Commenting on the results of the 1959 elections in Northern Nigeria, Kenneth Post writes, "There was no reason for the ruling groups in the emirates to become seriously alarmed after the election. For the great mass of the peasants their traditional authority still held good. . . . *Economic and social development still had far to go.*"[3] Unfortunately, this assumed incompatibility between "economic and social development" and "traditional authority" remains strong in the minds of many well-intentioned commentators—both expatriate and Nigerian—on the African political scene. Yet true development cannot proceed unless it is rooted in, and strengthened by, the culture (political and otherwise) whence it springs. Traditional rulers in Nigeria are no more antipathetic to development than are Nigerians in general; the question is, what *kind* of development is at stake, and what *kind* of political system will best facilitate the chosen path? This, Nigeria needs to decide for itself. The West may provide lessons, but it cannot serve as a model. *Nigeria itself*— tapping its own cultural wealth and diversity— must provide the model. It needs only the courage to look within.

Hassan Haruna, on democracy: "Men wander around like cattle, without any direction. . . . Each goes his own way, lost, until there's no more herd."

Campaign Songs

Transcribed from cassette by Lawal Nuhu; translated by Lawal Nuhu and the author.

NPN SONG

Chorus: **The Wily Ones Are Ashamed For Not Registering PPP [an NPN alliance group], No One Is More Conceited Than They.**

('Yan Samtsi Sun Ji Kunya PPP Ba Rijista Ba Sauran Hura Hanci.)

God is the Ultimate Ruler, He appoints His own ruler, Once He appoints his ruler, No one else may overthrow Him.

(Allah shi ke da mulki shi ne ke bada mulki muddin ya baka mulki ba mai nema ya kwace.)

Plateau state had great prosperity, until NPP took over, Then it was thrust into poverty.

(Plateau da mai arziki ce babba, da NPP ta kwace sun ka sasu cikin talauci.)

Look at their workers, They are not being paid,
They care for them, Then they ignore them,
They refuse to pay them their salaries, They show no respect.

*(Duba ga ma'aikatansu gama ba biyansu, sun
kulla sun ka barsu, albashi sun hana su
saboda rishin mutunci.)*

People of our nation, On voting day let us vote with care,
Let us reject our rivals, Who rule with disrespect.

*(Talakawan kasarmu ranar zabe mu zabi
muhimmi, mu ture mahassadanmu 'yan
mulkin cin mutunci.)*

NPP is nervous, confused, blind, It has no strength,
NPN will demolish it and establish a just administration.

*(NPP ta dimanta, ta rude, ta makanta ba wani
karfi gareta, NPN mukusheta ki kofa mulkin adalci.)*

What I have said is the truth, NPP are illiterates,
They are all old, poor people . . .

*(Zance na gaskiya ne NPP jahilai ne duk dattijan
tsiyane duba . . .)*

What I say applied to PPA [an opposition alliance] as well,
They are bastards, an evil congregation,
There isn't a decent person among them.

*(Ni zane na ya dace PPA shegiya ce mummunar
kungiya ce domin ciki ba dan mutunci.)*

Children, say it loud, PPA has lost its sons,
Expelled by their fathers for indecency.

*(Yara ku fada ku kara PPA tai sara 'ya'ya da
uba ya kora saboda rishin mutunci.)*

These thieves, who discriminate according to tribe,
They held a convention in Yola,
At it they said that all those who pray [i.e., Muslims]
Should be dealt with ruthlessly.

*(Barayi masu illa 'yan bambancin kabila sun wani
taro a Yola sun ce duk masu sallah sai sun masu
cin mutunci.)*

They want to bring changes to politics, But as hypocrites
They want NPN to fail,
But NPP will fail, and that will end their ingratitude.

*(Waisu canjin siyasa domin neman riyasu wai
NPN ta nisa NPP za ta kasa to mu ga karyar butulci.)*

His mother wears a cloth wrapper, His wife wears a cloth
    wrapper,
He too wears a cloth wrapper, The worthless one who treats
    others like dirt.

*(Uwar ta daura gyauto matar ta daura gyauto
shima ya daura gyauto dan banza mai cin mutunci.)*

Any NPP stalwart is a dog, As for me, if he dies,
Let him not be buried, Burn him in fire, The ingrate dog!

*(Duk dan samtsi kare ne ni dai da dai tani ne
in ya mutu kar a binne a kai shi wuta a kone kare
sarkin butulci.)*

Jatau [i.e., apparently Governor Rimi of Kano state], a slave to
    Jews, will teach your children to become effeminate,
To tie cloth wrappers round their hips like Dudu [i.e.,
    homosexuals],
A man of no virility.

*(Jatau bawan Yahudu zai koyawa diyanku
daudu su daura zane a kugu su
zarce su ga dudu ba da ne mai mutunci.)*

A dog that spoils prayer, Disobedient to God, this Jatau of Talata,
Whoever fasts and prays will reject him.

*(Kare mai karya sallah sarkin sabawa Allah,
Jatau gwarzon talata domin ajumi da sallah
bai mai kallon mutunci.)*

Fate has decreed that Kano elect a hypocrite,
An expert in cursing,
Satan the deviator, the King Ingrate.

(Ai komi kaddara ne Kano yau su fa gane sun
zabe munafiki ne gwanin Allah ya tsine
shaidan sarkin butulci.)

If you look closely, you will find that Maitatsine [the "False
    Prophet" who inspired unrest in Northern Nigeria] arose
    amongst the Governor's followers,
Jatau, the King Ingrate.

(An ma wani bincike ne bala'in Maitatsine ya
samu asali gun gwamnan 'yan tatsine Jatau sarkin
butulci.)

I wish to ask the husband of A'i, "Who sang this song?"
"Yakubu Labaran sang it, the junior brother of Ado and Binte,
A friend of NPN."

(Mijin A'i zan tambayaka, wakar nan wa ya yi ta?
Yakubu Labaran ya yi ta kannen Ado da Binta dan
NPN aminci.)

Rimi [i.e., the silk cotton tree, and also the name of the Kano
    governor, and NPP candidate] is brittle,
Its branch will impoverish you,
The son who abuses his father, who knows no respect.

(Rimi gautai gare shi reshe ne in ka bi shi
sai ya ja ma tsiyar shi ga mai zagin ubanshi
ba da ne mai mutunci.)

If I say "Governor," how can he be identified?
Rimi—a barren tree, a man of ingratitude.

(In na ce gwamna wane ta yaya za'a gane
Rimi iccen tsiyane ba— mutum ne koyar mai butulci.)

They had wanted to join NPN, But it refused, because of their evil
    mind,
With their leader Jatau, the King Profligate.

(Da sun jawo jikinsu sai NPN ta ki su domin
mugun halinsu da Jatau shugabansu sarkin 'yan
fasikanci.)

They decamped to NPP, The party of tyrants,
Dirty, just dirty, I went to them and I regretted it,
None worth being called a man.

(NPP sun ka koma jam'iyyar masu zulma, kazami
sai kazama na koma sai nadama ciki ba dan
mutunci.)

The inimical scorpion has decamped to NPP,
Just to obtain office,
For there is no self-respect.

(Tsinanne dan kunama wai NPP ya koma
yana neman mukama saboda rishin mutunci.)

True, some ran away from it, But Jatau has joined it,
All its supporters are bastards,
Don't support it, for within it there is no freedom.

('Yan sunna sun guje ta, ga Jatau ya shiga ya
duk shegu ne diyanta ga sunna kar ka yi ta
don ba yanci cikinta.)

Jatau, the crazy Governor, Whom will he impress?
Let me belittle the bastard, At every opportunity.

(Su Jatau gwamna wawa ya za ya birge kubarni in
goga shege bana tsoron ta shafe.)

We shall weigh the offence, Jatau the traitor,
To hell with the Governor, The profligate one.

(Laifi ne zamu auna Jatau mai cin amana Allah
tsinawa gwamnan mai yin fasikanci.)

Before, he was a decent sort, But he became an evil dog,
His time has come, the swindler of trust.

(Da dai mummuni ne ashe gwamnan tsiyane
Jatau mugun kare ne bakin ajjalumi ne mai
zamba cikin aminci.)

He provoked us, He abused Shagari, the father of our country,
Our faultless Helper.

(Shi ne za ya tsokanemu ya zagi uban kasarmu
Shagari mataimakinmu ba laifi.)

The people of Kano have realized that Maitatsine is no more,
But the Governor is Maitatsine's favorite,
He who commits sin.

(Kanawa sun fa gane an ce ba Maitatsine
nayan ga gwamna wane dangatan Maitatsine ya
yin fasikanci.)

Bashir Walin, our Governor [i.e., NPN candidate],
You are a Patriot, For God's sake push out Governor Jatau,
The traitor, the ingrate.

(Bashir Walin mu gwamna kai dan kishin kasa ne
do Allah ture gwamna Jatau mai cin amana
shaidan sarkin butulci.)

I used to be on the Arabic side [i.e., with Aminu Kano],
Thinking there, there is peace,
But I didn't know I was stepping on a scorpion,
PRP is tyrannical, and power hungry.

(Da dai Arabic na kama nai tsammanin salama ashe
na hau dan kunama PRP sai zalama da hadamar
shugabanci.)

PRP steals, Its followers are pickpockets,
With it, you see two fingers,
Pickpocketing never brings wealth,
It only brings poverty.

(PRP na da sata 'yan sani ne cikinta yatsu
biyu in ka ganta sani bai sai wadata sai
dai karin talauci.)

That's why I ran away from it, Because I don't steal,
I returned to the upright NPN,
The party of goodness and decency.

(Shi ya sa na guje ta domin ni ba ne sata na
koma gun nagarta NPN na aminta jami'iyyar yan
mutunci.)

Everybody has understood that there is kindness in NPN,
If you follow it you will become an upright son, Who respects the
  rights of others.

*(Yau komw ya fahinta alheri ke cikinta NPN in
ka bi ta ka zama da mai nagarta ka sau hakkin
mutunci.)*

People, you have seen the impoverished GNPP,
NPP has scattered.

(Talakawa ku gane GNPP tsiya ne NPP sai su ware.)

Oh, understanding child, come to NPN and rest,
It is kind,
I myself am enriched, I am not poor.

*(Ya kai da mai fahinta zo NPN ka huta
don alheri gareta, ni ma nan na wadata
domin ba ne talauci.)*

Today, everybody has understood,
The whole country is enriched,
Because NPN is generous,
NPN followers are not profligate.

*(Yau kowa ya fahinta kasa duk an wadata domin
kirki gareta NPN sahibanta ba mai yin fasikanci.)*

NPP SONGS

Chorus: **"NPN!" [as response to questions]**

Who increased the price of Omo [detergent], soap, and body
  cream?

*(Wa ya kara kudin Omo da sabulu da mai mai
guguwa?)*

Who brought Ojukwu [leader of the Biafra secession, pardoned
  by President Shagari in 1983] into the country to reveal his
  meanness?

*(Wa ya zo da Ojukwu kasar domin ya tashi yai ta
halin tsiya?)*

Who went to Togo, drank alcohol, and grabbed Magajiya [i.e., a
woman]?

(Wa ya je shi Togo ya sha giya ya kama Magajiya?)

He grabbed her buttocks, She said, "Stop it, old man!"

(Ya kama duwawunta ta ce da shi dattijo ya dakata.)

He said, "Wait and listen, I am the president of Nigeria!"

(Sai ya ce ki tsaya ki ji ni ne fa shugaban Nijeriya.)

The president of Nigeria, Who absconds with the money.

(Shugaban Nijeriya shi ne ya kwashe kudin dukiya.)

Praise our Kano Governor Rimi, Who does not like destitution.

*(Kai mu gode Gwamna na Kanonmu Rimi wanda ba
ya son tsiya.)*

Who creates hardship for the masses in this country?

*(Bai cin ba kasar nan ne wa ya baiwa talakawa
wuya?)*

The Chairman of Danbatta is not wicked, Habu of Danbatta is
not wicked.

*(Cayaman Danbatta ga shi ba ya son tsiya, Habu na
Danbatta wallahi shi fa ba ya son tsiya.)*

Let us sleep in Danbatta, The town that does not like poverty.

*(Kai mu kwana a Danbatta yau ga garin da ba son
tsiya.)*

Oh, let us sleep in Danbatta, The town where there is no
selfishness.

*(Kai mu kwana a Danbatta yau ga garin da ba son
zuciya.)*

As for me, I too believe Rimi works selflessly.

(Ni na yarda aikinka Rimi bai son zuciya.)

He developed the city, He developed the countryside, No hardship there.

(Ya gyara garin birni ya gyara karkara ba shan wuya.)

Who took over this country, and caused petrol to be scarce?

(Wa ya karbe kasar nan ne ya san ya mai na fetur yai wuya?)

They burned the building of Lagos, and made off with so much wealth.

(Sun kone ginin Lagos sun ka kwashe dinbin dukiya.)

They burned our Abuja, and made off with the wealth.

(Sun kone Abujanmu sun kwashe dinbin dukiya.)

The presidency of this country, God knows, will not be given to the selfish one.

(Mulki dai ne kasar nan wallahi bamu baiwa mai tsiya.)

Come '83, we shall never give in to the selfish one.

(In '83 ta za ba mu bai wa mai son zuciya.)

Who killed people during the Premier's time [i.e., First Republic] because of rivalry?

(Wa ya karkeshe jama'a a zamanin firimiya kan gaba?)

Who killed people, but still he is free [reference to Ojukwu]?

(Wa ya karkashe jama'a a kasar nan amman yanzu ya nan tsaye?)

But now NPN says Nigeria will go with him, They even gave him a title.

(Amma yanzu ko NPN ta ce da shi Nijeriya har ta bashi mukami.)

To hell with you, niggardly ones!

(Allah wadanku masu halin tsiya!)

Our leaders are whisky drunkards,
We have to tell you "Enough!"

(Malamanmu na 'yan whisky wallahi sai mu ce kaka an isa.)

Our whisky leader, let us tell you, God suffices for us.

(Shugabanmu na 'yan whisky sai mu ce fa ai Allah ya isa.)

You took our money to Togo, You enjoyed it in your meanness.

(Ka kwashe kudin namu je ka Togo ka yi halin tsiya.)

You went to Togo, drank wine and held a woman.

(Ka je fa Togo ka sha giya san nan fa ka kama Magajiya.)

He held her buttocks, He stroked her breast,
The wicked one.

(Ya kama duwaiwanta ya shafa mama mai halin tsiya.)

You old man, Why do you behave so badly?

(Kai dattijo yaya ka ke fa halin tsiya?)

"Wait and hear, I am the president of Nigeria."

(Ai ki tsaya ki ji ni ne fa shugaban Nijeriya.)

You have embezzled our wealth, You have left the masses in hardship.

*(Ku da fa kun kwashe dinbin dukiya ku ku ka bar
talakawanku ko wa ne na halin wuya.)*

With five jets you went to Kano, campaigning.

(Ku ku je yakin zabe Kano jirgin sama jai biyar.)

You went campaigning, with jets hanging in the air.

(Kun je yakin zabe jirgin sama sun tsaya.)

You took our money, and bought jets.

*(Ku ka kwashe kudin namu ku ka saye jirage don
tsiya.)*

Our whiskey leader, we say to you,
For us, God is sufficient.

*(Shugabanmu na 'yan whiskey mu sai mu ce maka
Allah ya isa.)*

You will never rule this country again.

(Ba zaku fa kara rikon kasar Nijeriya.)

Azikiwe, our man, he is a ruler for Nigeria . . .

(Ga Azikiwe namu she ne fa mai rikon Nijeriya.)

Chorus: NPN, An Arena of Fraud!

(NPN Dandalin Zamba.)

A hyena is not used to justice,
A hyena is selfish.

*(Kura ba ta saba rikon amana ba.
To dai ita kura tafi son kanta.)*

It is asked to share something equally,
Then asked not to be selfish.

(Sai aka bata rabo ta daidaita.
An ce don Allah kar ta sa cuta.)

But it does not know justice,
It divided it into three, and then held it.

(Amma ita ko ba ta san adalci ba.
Wai sai ta kasa uku duk ta kakkama.)

It said, "This portion is for hyena,
This portion is for scavenger,
And the remaining portion is to be fought after."

(Amma ta ce wannan na kura ne.
Wannan kashi daya ko na mai dare ne.
Ai to kun ji kashi daya ko na wawa ne.)

Nobody will beat her to it . . .

(Ai ba za'a riga ta diba ba.)

Respect your power, policemen,
If not you will find out,
Soldiers and police are excluded from politics.

(Gane ku ja girmanku 'yan sanda.
Amma in kun ki kuwa za'a takaku.
Lalle fa ba soja bare fa 'yan sanda.)

But one soldier intervenes [Obasanjo?].
Call him a leader in fraud . . .

(Amma wani fa soja ya dago baki.
To sai mu kira shi da shugaban zamba.)

Oh, Akinloye and Shagari,
They are not good sons.

(Waiyo da Akinloye shi da Shagari.
Ka san ba 'ya'ya ne na kirki ba.)

If you just chat with them, they'll go mad,
They'll go and look for stars,
Or he'll ride in the air to eat cassava flour . . .

(Sai a taba su kadan su hau bori.
Kuma har sun je sun duba taurari.
Ko ya hau sama don ya sha gari.)

There is a Divisional Police Officer,
Patting his belly like a big pot.

(Da akwai wani DPO na'yan sanda.
Ya daure cikinsa kamar uwar sanda.)

He did not put on his uniform properly.
He arrested us one day at Hadeja's.

(Wanda ko damarar ya kasa daurawa.
Ran nan fa Hadejia shi ya kama mu.)

I called him a leader in fraud.
As soon as you left, he arrested us . . .

(To sai na kira shi da shugaban zamba.
Da dai tafiyarmu guri ya kama mu.)

You know that NPN has three factions.

(Kun san fa ita NPN kashi uku ce.)

NPN is for the past.
NPN is for inheritance.
NPN is for madness.

(Kun san fa NPN ta dai da ce.
San nan ita NPN ta gado ce.
Kun san fa wata NPN ta hauka ce.)

Never will we join it.

(Har abada ba zamu nufa ba ciki yi ba.)

Chorus: **NPP is the Party of Change, to the Masses Does It
Give Just Due.**

(Jam'iyyar Canji NPP Mai Fitar Da Hakkin Talakawa.)

You who want power, I want to remind you,
They have ruled in the past, What have they done for us?
We the masses have suffered.

(Ku masu son mulki zan tuna maku masu son mulki
shekaru can baya sun mulki mi suka yi mana?
Sun wahalar da mu jama'a talakawa.)

I like Danbatta, For there Reza surprised me,
By urging people to consider the era we are living in.

(Danbatta nai sha'awa, a nan Reza ta ban shawa
ta soma fada a nan sai ta ce jama'a ku bari
ku dubi zamanin da muke talakawa.)

God the ruler, Formerly we were in PRP,
But now we have decamped,
We are in NPP, The party that gives the people rights.

(Allahu mai iko, mu da fa muna ta PRP, yanzu mun
yi mun kare, karshe kuma mun kare a yanzu mu na
NPP mai son kwato hakkin jama'a talakawa.)

Don't slack, Muhammadu Rimi, Let us unite and leave no stone
unturned,
Let us finish off the bastard Wali supporters.

(Rimi kar ka sake, Muhammadu Rimi, kar mu bar
kofa a kasa, mu karye 'yan laka 'yan Wali.)

They are blundering,
They went to Danbatta, Kazaure, Minjibir, Gazewa.
Holding rallies, Asking the people to vote for them,
Saying, "Surely Kano is for Wali,"
But Omo is costly, Kano now is smelling [a Hausa play on the
       words *Wali*, the NPN candidate, and *wari*, meaning "stench"],
We are in NPP, Let the people come and join Rimi.

(Suna da yin shirme, su je yawan su Danbatta
da Kazaure su je su Danbatta Munjibir har
ma su Gazewa suna yawo suna lacca suna
jama'a ku zabemu, Wallahi fa Kano sai Wali,
ashe haka zaku ce jama'a domin Omo ya na tsada
ai yanzu Kano fa sai Wari to muko yanzu sai
canji jama'a ta za mu gushe sai Rimi.)

No bathing, no washing,
Omo is costly,
We must say Kano is stinking.

> (Ba a yin wanka ba wani sabulu tsada zuwa Omo
> ai dole ku ce da mu jama'a sai wari.)

We want change now,
All the people want change,
Men and women, our children too,
Are shouting "Give us Rimi, Give us change!"

> (Mu yanzu sai canji, talakawa duk yi canji,
> maza, matanmu canji yaranmu fada suka canji sai
> Rimi.)

At resting places and during weddings,
People are shouting for change,
Others don't want change,
But God will change life for the people,
And we will be happy.

> (A wurin wuni canji, a wajen aure canji amma
> wasu ba su son canji, Allah canja zaman
> jama'a mu ji dadi.)

Think about it,
Nowadays the five kobo coin is rare,
Only one naira, and twenty naira notes are in circulation,
Three pence coins are good for nothing.

> (Ai yanzu ba sisi, in kun lura sisi sai muna
> naira, sai fam goma sule naira da fam goma
> balle wali taron sisi, balle walin da taro girman
> banza.)

University students, help us,
For we are the ones who bring change for the masses.

> (Mu dalibai namu na kasarmu jami'oinmu University
> masu kannarmu ku tsaya ku tsamo mu tun da
> mune muka canjin talakawa.)

When Mallam [Aminu Kano] was alive,
We came to you students for help,
But you were afraid of him,

Now that he is dead,
And the governor has decamped from PRP,
All the people are for Rimi.

*(Ai tun da ran Mallam, muna magana da ran
Mallam dalibai mun zo ku cecemu kuna tsoron
halin Mallam to yanzu gashi ba Mallam kuma
gwamnan gashi ba PRP dukkan jama'a sai Rimi.)*

The masses love us,
Tell our supporters that they should vote,
For the Governor who loves the masses.

*(Ku ku ke sonmu talakawa ku ku ke sonmu,
ku fadawa duk masoyanmu kuriarku ku sakawa
gwamna mai son talakawa.)*

He who wants to climb a tree should get a ladder or rope,
Rimi is the people's choice.

*(Kai kuma mai hawan bishiya tafi nemi abin
hawa bishiyar, ko tsani ko ka sa igiya abin
hawa bisiya da Rimi mai jama'a talakawa.)*

He [Rimi] works to develop the country,
The rulers spend money,
But the workers aren't paid,
The masses are suffering.

*(Ga wanda zai aiki domin gyaran kasarsu yaka
a kashe kurdi bisa aiki, ba'a sami ba kurdi
ba aiki jama'a na shan bakar wahalla talakawa.)*

On election day the masses should study and vote,
For the person who will fight for their rights.

*(Ba a ba kuri'a talakawa za a zaba sai ku yi
nazari wajen jefa kuri'a, kuri'arku ku ba mai
son jama'a mai son kwato hakkin jama'a talakawa.)*

I am not flattering you, the masses,
I am saying what I know about you,
Our motto is, "We love the people."

*(Ba zuge ba nike talakawa ba zuge ba nike, ni
halinku nike fada manufarmu mu so jama'a
talakawa.)*

I am warning the masses,
Don't play with your votes.

*(Gargadinku nike talakawa gargadinku nike don
kar da ku shantake ku sake har ya saku ku sake
kuri'arku ya sa ku sake talakawa.)*

Right is with them,
The people know who is a traitor,
Let us join hands and help the masses.

*(Don alhakin jama'a na nan a garesu, ku jama'a
tun da dai kun san mai ki jama'a to mu taro mu
taimaka ma jama'a talakawa.)*

NPN doesn't want change,
They don't even want to hear the word,
But NPP is the party that brings change.

*(Ba su son canji NPN ba su son canji
a fada a'a, to NPP jami'yyar canji.)*

Don't ignore the monkey who destroys,
Who refuses to give people their due,
And the due of the nation.

*(Kar ku baiwa biri mai barna wanda zai kare
hakkin jama'ar kasa ya tsare hakkin kasa
bai kula ba da hakkin talakawa.)*

And don't ignore the hyena,
Whose aim is to scorn all others,

(Kuma kar ku bai kura, burin kua ya saye ya tsare.)

It is not the intention of NPP,
That the children of Nigeria should grow up uneducated.

*(Ai ba nufinta ba ne NPP yaranmu su ta shi ba su
sani, yaronmu su girma ba su sani a cikin Nijeriya
talakawa.)*

[NPP] wants everyone to stand on his own,
It doesn't want anyone to step on thorns,
NPP wants everyone to stand on his own,
So that we, the masses, don't step on thorns.

> *(Ita so taka ku tsaya, ga maza ma so taka ku
> tsaya kowa da katarsa zaya tsaya kar mu
> yi ratsa mu taka kaya, NPP so ta ke mu
> tsaya kar mu yi ratsa mu tka kaya talakawa.)*

Muhammadu Rimi, son of Garba,
You aim to develop knowledge, education,
May God help you,
The man who loves the masses.

> *(Muhammadu Rimi dan Garba, niyarka ta raya ilmi,
> Allah ya nufeka dan Garba mai son mu mutan
> kasa jama'a talakawa.)*

The tyrants who kill us, They stole our father's money,
Then they beat us,
When we talk about it, They don't like it,
But we refuse to be quiet, We must say it.

> *(Yau ga macutanmu wadanda suke kashe cemu
> sun sace kudin iyayyenmu suke dokemu da
> ga cewa ai ku dokemu ba su son magana tuni mun ki.)*

Habu the Chairman in Danbatta,
Tijani the Councilor, Well done,
He too is a freedom fighter.

> *(Habu na Danbatta Chayaman na Danbatta, Councilla
> Tijani direba na gode, Tijani dai gaisheka nai
> son kwato hakkin jama'a shi ma.)*

Thank you Sani the Driver,
Haji the Glass Man, Muhammadu our Director,
May God change the way of the nation,
So that we, the people, are happy.

> *(Sani direba na gode, Haji Musa namu mai tasa,
> Muhammadu namu direkita Allah canja zaman
> kasa jama'a mu ji dadi.)*

Leave no door ajar,
Let us unite and leave no stone unturned,
This year we, the people, must win.

*(Yau kar mu bar kofa, talakawa kar mu bar
kofa mu hada kai mu bar kofa kasa duka
mai kofa bana sai mun kai ga cin nasara talakawa.)*

Our party is NPP,
NPN is a jealous party,
They throw away their money,
They bribe the emir, the Village Head, the Ward Head . . .

*(Ai jami'yyarmu ita ce NPP, NPN jami'yyar huzinu,
su suka zubda kurdinsu suka sai sarki da kurdinsu
ka sai dagaci da kurdinsu da ka sai mai unguwa.)*

PRP SONG

If a party has won two states already, It may rule the entire
country [reference to PRP in Kano and Kaduna states].

*(Duk mai neman mulkin kasarmu ya samu sita biyu
ya yi samu.)*

In the time it takes to sleep and awake,
We shall rule the whole of the nation.

*(To kan ana kwana a tashi za ya mallaki dukkan
kasarmu.)*

A friend of Hassan [Yusufu, PRP presidential candidate after
Aminu Kano's death] is leading our country,
And we hope that he takes our brother's advice.

*(Goga na Hassan shugaba wanda ke jagorar
kasarmu. Amma muna fata ya gane ya dauki nasiha
'yanuwanmu.)*

A hen never gets angry with its chick,
But trods on it until it dies.

*(Ai kaza ba ta fushi da danta ta tattakeshi
ya je kiyama.)*

Truth is bitter, He who speaks it,
Must endure what his enemies say.

*(To gaskiya ita kam daci gare ta mai fadarta
ya gure 'yan husuma.)*

He will face opposition, Let him be calm,
Some will even come fight him.

*(Zai sha zargi sai dai ya daure, wasu ma har
su nemai da husuma.)*

I, the son of Hauwa'u, Amina's junior brother,
I will say it, even if we are to be beaten.

*(Ni dan Hauwa'u kanan Amina zan fada ko da
wani zai buge mu.)*

Oh, people, I want to ask a question,
Answer me, for God's sake.

*(Ni shi jama'a zan tambayeku ku ban amsa don
wanda yayi mu.)*

Is it the people who make up a market,
Or stalls without tomatoes [i.e., empty].

*(Taron jama'a ne kasuwa ko yawan rumfa ba
mai tumatir?)*

A market is made up of people,
And the market is here with us.

*(Taron jama'a ne kasuwa, kasuwar kun ganta
tana garemu.)*

Oh people, come to the market,
Come to help the rest of our brothers.

*(Jama'a ku taho ku ci kasuwa don a taimaki
sauran 'yanuwanmu.)*

Oh people, come to the market, so that he
Who hasn't got will get.

(To jama'a ku taho ku ci kasuwa wanda ba
ya da shi shi ma ya samu.)

There are Imo state people, Bandelites, Rivers,
And Cross Rivers people,
All these people are with us.

(Ga mutanen Imo da Bendel da Rivers da
Cross Rivers cikinmu.)

There are people from Kwara, Cross Rivers,
Bendelites and Bauchi right behind us.

(Ga mutanen Kwara da Cross Rivers da Bendel
da Bauchi sun biyamu.)

There are people of Yola among us,
Bauchi people,
All together, backing us.

(Ga mutanen Yola sun cikinmu na Bauchi
gaba daya sun biyamu.)

Sokoto, Kaduna junction and Kano,
They've come and are with us.

(Ga Sakkwato su Kaduna juntshun da Kanon mu
ta Dabo suna cikinmu.)

If a porridge hawker doesn't sell her porridge,
Let her husband buy it,
Let them dilute it.

(Wai mai fura kan ba ta san kasuwa ba mijin
ya saye su rabka damu.)

NPN is not sold in Kano,
Take it to Gusau
Take it to Gurmi [both in Sokoto state].

(NPN a Kano bata san saye ba maye
ta Gusau a kaita Gurmi.)

Let us unite, oh brothers,
Let us help the rest of our brothers.

*(Mu hada kai ya ku 'yanuwanmu don a
taimaki sauran 'yanuwanmu.)*

Together we can change our country,
Our motherland.

*(Don kuwa sai da hada kai za mu samu a
canja kasarmu ta haihuwarmu.)*

Unity may not guarantee prosperity,
But disunity will not bring it, either.

*(Ai kan hadin kai ba zama arziki ba
rabuwa tasa ba ta sa a samu.)*

For unity is an aim,
Which will finish off our traitors,

*(Don kuwa hadin kai babbar garkuwarmu wanda
za ya gama da mayaudaranmu.)*

Patience is our bomb,
Which will demolish our traitors.

*(Hakuri kuwa shi ne bam garemu zai rugurguza
duk mayaudaranmu.)*

Now our rivals see us ruling,
We the people, who are making changes.

*(Ai yanzu da makiyanmu suna gani muna
mulkin suna ganinmu.)*

We, the people who are making changes, deserve recognition,
Oh people, don't let it slip away from us.

*(Mu ne mu ke canjin da ake yabonmu
jama'a kar mu sake ya barmu.)*

But the leaders of the others are imitating us,
Now they know that we are better than they.

*(Mu mu ke aikin da a ke yabon mu shugaban
wasu har ya kwaikwayemu. Ai yanzu dai sun
san mun fi su tsari yadda.)*

We shall work so that all the people prefer us,
All our governors are intelligent,
They know the disease in our body.

> *(Za mu yi har jama'a ta so mu. Ai duka*
> *gwamnoninmu akwai basira su su ka san*
> *cutar jikinmu.)*

The doctor who knows the disease in your body,
He will cure you quickly.

> *(Dakita da ya san cutar jikinka maganin*
> *sauri za kai ka samu.)*

For many years in the country,
The sickness within us wanted to kill us.

> *(Ai shekara da yawa a cikin kasa cuta*
> *a jikinmu ta zo ta karmu.)*

People, you knew the sickness in us,
But they wanted it to kill us.

> *(Jama'a ku san cutar jikinmu sun*
> *yarda ta zo ta karmu.)*

Previously cattle tax and poll tax,
Wanted to ruin our country.

> *(Da jangalin dabba da biya haraji ya so ya*
> *kashe kasarmu.)*

Inheritance tax wanted to kill,
And ruin our country.

> *(Ushiran mutuwa kan auyi gado ta*
> *so ta kashe mu ta kar kasarmu.)*

Loincloth and helmet should be removed,
And dumped in a ditch [unpopular laws requiring the wearing of
motorcycle helmets were repealed by PRP].

> *(Darmin cinya hula ta kwano ta ce mu*
> *fitar mu zuba a rami.)*

Oh people, I want to ask you a question,
Answer me, for God's sake.

*(Ni shin jama'a zan tambayeku ku ban amsa
don wanda ya yi mu.)*

What is a son struggling to get in this,
And the next world?

*(Mi da ke fafutukar ya samu duniya kan
komawar kiyama?)*

High standing in their country has unfettered them,
Don't let it cause us misfortune.

*(A martaba a karsarsu ya samu 'yanci girmawa
kadda a tsangwamemu.)*

Now in Kano we are free, Nobody will fail us,
Much less beat us.

*(Ai yanzu mu a Kano mun sami 'yanci babu
mai dauremu ya bugagemu.)*

We cannot be maltreated on account of taxes,
We cannot be beaten because we haven't paid.

*(Mun zarce walakancin haraji a kan mu
biya sai an bugemu.)*

We are not forced to till someone's field,
Or carry wood beams without pay.

*(Ba mu yin noman gandu a tilas ko mu
dauki azara babu gammo.)*

We of Kano cannot be mistreated,
For God has helped us.

*(Mu yan Kanawa mun wuce cin mutunci tunda
dai Allah ya taimakemu.)*

Who said we are free, Stop jailing us,
Stop beating us?

(Ai su wa suka ce mun sami 'yanci
a bar dauremu ana bugarmu?)

Who brought pipe-borne water,
Electricity which lights up in the bush?

(Wai su wa su ka kai fanfo, latirin 'yan
haske a kauye?)

Look at the motor tracks,
Every street in every village will be tarred.

(Ga titainan mota ko wane kauye za'a sa
kwalto ya 'yanuwanmu.)

Jallof rice, pounded yam and meat,
Don't let hunger kill us.

(Yau dafa duka ga sakwara da nama kar
mu bari yunwa ta karmu.)

Let's talk of porridge and sour milk,
Don't let us suffer.

(Yin fadawa ga fa dawa da nono kar ku
bari har ku yi gama.)

Let the Bauchi people come,
There are some cakes with stew.

(Bauchi sai ku taho ga masa an taushe
an savya nama.)

Here is millet couscous for Borno,
With stew and meat.

(To Borno ga burabisko an yi miya an
sauya nama.)

For Jos people yam porridge is finished,
Meat is added.

(To ko Jos an kare fate da doya an kara
an sauya nama.)

Gongola state is full of milk, Let them drink it,
And fry the meat.

*(Gongola kasarsu suna da nono su sha
nononsu su soya nama.)*

Benue and Makurdi have yam,
Cook it and add meat to it.

*(Benue da Makurdi suna da doya a dafa ta
a sauya mata nama.)*

You, Kwara, buy aigo and pound it,
Get stew and meat.

*(To ku Kwara ku sai aigo ku kirba ku yi
miyankuku sauya nama.)*

The Yorubas prefer eba,
When eating it, you stroke your beard.

*(Yarabawa teba suke bukata kan kana ci
ka ga shafa gemu.)*

For Igbos, they prefer boiled yam,
Even without meat.

*(A wajen Igbo su kam gwara doya a dafata baka
ko babu nama.)*

Let the Hadejia people take pumpkin,
Even without groundnuts and meat.

*(Hadeja ku sha tabshen kabewa ko babu
gyada ko babu nama.)*

Come people, hear the word of the secret language,
And its meaning.

*(Yaku jama'ar mana kun ji kalma mai kamar
zaurance ko alama.)*

Our aim is to be understood, Oh brothers.

(Manufarmu a nan don ku gane ya
ku jama'a ga 'yanuwanmu.)

In the upcoming elections, Vote for PRP
So as not to regret your choice.

(Zaben gaba kan za'a sake ku zabi
PRP kar ku nadama.)

It has brought changes that have made
The other parties jealous.

(Ai yanzu ta zo da canji wanda ya sauya
maza nadama.)

Vote for PRP so as to change the nation,
So as to improve the country.

(Ku zabi PRP ko kuwa ga canji ko a
gyara zaman kasarmu.)

Here is a house with a poster,
Look, what is the symbol?

(Yau ga gida da takarda jikinsu gano mana
mi suka sa alama.)

They drew a house without a gate,
With corn sprouting a "beard" [i.e., fiber on the ear].

(Wai su gida suka zana babu kofa da dan
masara ya fidda gemu.)

An ear of corn is shameless,
Like a child, it is carried on its mother's back,
But it sprouts a beard.

(Shi dan masara dai bai da kunya ana
goyonsa ya fidda gemu.)

Now if that isn't the height of shamelessness . . .
It is madness and nonsense to have corn as a symbol.

*(In ban da maras kunya tsururu ana goyonka
ka fidda gemu. In ban da ma hauka da rashin
basira da dan masara za a yi alama.)*

We shall pluck the corn, break its ear,
Throw it into the fire, and burn the "beard."

*(Mu mun cire masara mun karya danta
a sake a wuta mu kone gemu.)*

Let us not be ensnared by the enemy,
Traitors of the people, traitors of our country!

*(To kar mu yarda da zargin an adawa mukiyan
jama'a mukiya kasarmu.)*

It was dark, only now has dawn broken,
We see our hero.

*(Yau an dare sai yanzu gari ya waye muka
gane dan kishin kasarmu.)*

We see our patriots, Those who love the nation,
Oh, God bless the patriots,
And those who love the nation.

*(Mu ka gane 'yan kishin kasarmu wadanda suka
kaunar kasarmu. Allah wadanda suka kishin
kasarmu wadanda suka kaunar kasarmu.)*

Glossary of Hausa Political Terminology

Typographical exigencies preclude utilizing the "hooked" Hausa consonants of "b," "d," and "k."

adalci	justice
addini	religion
alhaji	one who has made the pilgrimage to Mecca; title for a rich or important person
alkali	judge
alkawari	promise; affirmation
amana	trust
aminci	friendship
Annasara	white man; Christian (pl. *Nasarawa*)
arziki	wealth
attajiri	merchant (pl. *attajirai*)
bakin fata	black person
bara	client, servant
barantaka	clientship
Bature	European (pl. *Turawa*)
bauta	servitude
bautawa kasa	serving the state
bayani	speech, statement
bidi'a	a rebel, rebellion; heresy
bindiga	gun, firearm
birni	city
biyayya	obedience
butulci	ingratitude
canji	change
cayaman	chairman
chapka	loyalty, allegiance

cika magana	keep one's word, fulfill a promise
cin amana	betrayal
cin hanci	bribery
cin mutumci	humiliation, indignity, disrespect
cuta	deceit, cheating
dagaci	village area head (pl. *dagatai*)
daji	bush, countryside
damaji	damaged (invalid) ballot
dan majalisa	representative; councilor (pl. *'yan majalisa*)
dan sanda	police
dan siyasa	politician
daraja	rank, standing
dimokuradiyya	democracy
dogari	palace (emir's) guard (pl. *dogarai*)
doka	law, rule (pl. *dokoki*)
dolle	necessity
dubara	plan, idea; scheme, device, trick
duhu	darkness, ignorance
dukiya	wealth, asset
dukiya kasa	national prosperity
farin ciki	happiness
farin fula	civilian
farin jini	popularity
fasikanci	profligacy; immorality
Filanin gida	town-Fulani; Fulani ruling class
gado	inherited (ascriptive) status
gaisuwa	greeting; salute; gift presented to superior
galadima	adviser to the chief or emir
gama-kai	self-help; mutual assistance; cooperation
gargadi	warning, reprimand
gargajiya	tradition, olden times and ways; indigenous
gari	town, settlement (pl. *garuruwa*)
gaskiya	truth
girma	prestige, importance
girman kai	pride, conceit, arrogance
godiya	thankfulness
goyon baya	support
gunduma	village area (administrative district)
gurguzu	communism
gwamna	governor (pl. *gwamnoni*)
gwamnati	government
Habe	indigenous (i.e., non-Fulanized) Hausa
ha'inci	fraud, deceit
hakimi	district head (pl. *hakimai*)
hakki	due, right
hakuri	patience
halal	legitimate

hamiyya	opposition
haraji	poll tax
haram	unlawful (according to Islamic law)
haske	light, enlightenment
hauka	madness
Hausa Bakwai	seven (original) Hausa families
ijma	social consensus
iko	power, authority, control
ilmi	education, knowledge, learning
intabiyu	interview
iyyaka	border
izni	authority
jahilci	ignorance
jama'a	community, public
jamhuriya	republic
jamiyya	political party; club; association; movement
jangali	cattle tax
jiha	state (pl. *jihohi*)
jihad	holy war to spread Islam
kabila	tribe, ethnic group
kabilanci	tribalism
kai ya waiye	become (politically) conscious
kamu	arrest
kantoma	local government administrator (pl. *kantomomi*)
karamci	generosity
karamin hukuma	local government area, district
karya	lie, falsehood
kasa	country, region, emirate, area (pl. *kasashe*)
kauye	village, bush, countryside (pl. *kauyuka*)
kirki	honesty, virtue
kishin kasa	patriotism, nationalism
kokari	effort, striving
kotu	court
kudi	money
kumya	shame, embarrassment
kungiya	society, association, club
kunya	(see *kumya*)
kuri'a	ballot, vote (pl. *kuri'o'i*)
lacca	lecture
ladabi	proper demeanor, manners, politeness; obedience
lafiya	health, good condition, well-being
laifi	crime, fault, offense
lalaci	spoiled, ruined
limam	Koranic priest (pl. *limamai*)
liman	(see *limam*)
ma'aji	treasurer
magaji	princely heir

mai-gari	village chief (pl. *masu-gari*)
mai-gunduma	village area head
mai-karya	liar
mai-kudi	wealthy person (pl. *masu-kudi*)
mai-neman zabe	candidate
mai-taimakon	
shugaban kasa	vice-president
mai-unguwa	ward head
mai-zabe	elector
majalisa	legislature; council
majalisa dinkin	
duniya	United Nations
majilisa	(see *majalisa*)
mallam	Koranic teacher (pl. *mallamai*)
manufofi	platform
manya-manya	"big shots," important people; upper class
maroki	praise-singer (pl. *maroka*)
mukami	traditional title
mulki	rule, regime; control
mulkin farin fula	civilian rule
mulkin kai	self-government, independence
mulkin soja	military rule
mulkin Turawa	European or colonial rule, era
mullaka	rule, govern, have authority over
munafunci	hypocrisy
murdiya	twisting, corruption
mutumin kirki	good man
mutunci	respect, decency, dignity
nadawa	appointment, turbaning, nomination
Nasara	(see *Annasara*)
nasara	victory
neman zabe	campaign
pawa	power
ra'ayi	opinion, point of view
rabo	luck, fortune, success, fate; part, share
raino	care for, nurse; colonize
rangadi	tour
raya kasa	development
rishin kunya	shamelessness
roka	praise
rowa	avarice, miserliness
samariya	youth club
sanarwa	announcement, notice, warning
saraki	member of royalty
sarakuna	rulers
sarakuna na	
gargajiya	traditional rulers

sarauta	titled office; political position
sardauna	royal title of Sokoto
sarki	emir, king, chief (pl. *sarakuna, sarakai*)
Sarkin Mussulmi	"King of the Muslims," sultan of Sokoto
shari'a	Koranic law
shigege	achieved status
shugaba	leader
shugaban kasa	president (pl. *shugabanni kasa*)
siyasa	politics
soja	soldier (pl. *sojoji*)
soji	(see *soja)*
soyayya	mutual affection
talaka	commoner, peasant (pl. *talakawa*)
talauci	poverty
taro	assembly, meeting
tashin hankali	senselessness; violence
tattalin arziki	economy
tsarin mulki	constitution
tsegumi	slander
tsiya	destitution, poverty; quarrelsomeness
Turanci	English, "European" language
umurni	authorization; instruction
unguwa	ward, quarter (of village or town) (pl. *ungowyi*)
wahala	suffering
wakili	senator; deputy; agent (pl. *wakilai*)
walwala	happiness
wayo	cunning
wofi	useless, good-for-nothing; decadence
wulakanta	treachery
yaki	war
'yanci	independence, freedom
'yan iska	ragamuffins, hooligans, disaffected urban youth
yarjejeniya	agreement; treaty; reconciliation
zabe	election, vote
zage-zage	insult
zalunci	tyranny
zaman lafiya	peace, prosperity
zamani	modern; epoch, time, period
zamba	fraud, swindling, embezzling

Notes

PREFACE

1. Larry Diamond, "A Tarnished Victory for the NPN?," *Africa Report* (November–December 1983); "The Coup and the Future," *Africa Report* (March–April 1984); "Nigeria in Search of Democracy," *Foreign Affairs* 62 (Spring 1984).
2. Richard Joseph, "The Overthrow of Nigeria's Second Republic," *Current History* 83 (1984).
3. Kenneth Post and Michael Vickers, *Structure and Conflict in Nigeria, 1960–1966* (Madison: University of Wisconsin Press, 1973), 6.
4. Margaret Peil, *Nigerian Politics: The People's View* (London: Cassell, 1976), 3.
5. Ibid., 2.

CHAPTER 1: THE SETTING

1. This was in 1983. Upon taking power in 1984, the military abolished the Zango local government area, and with it the position of *kantoma*.

CHAPTER 2: THE "DEMOCRATIZATION" OF DAURA

1. Much of this chapter is subsequently based on C. S. Whitaker, *The Politics of Tradition: Continuity and Change in Northern Nigeria, 1946–1966* (Princeton: Princeton University Press, 1970) and M. G. Smith, *The Affairs of Daura: History and Change in a Hausa State, 1800–1958* (Berkeley: University of California Press, 1978).
2. Robert Heussler, "Indirect Rule in Northern Nigeria," *South Atlantic Quarterly* 47 (1968): 506.

3. Whitaker, *Politics of Tradition*, 55.
4. Ibid., 467.
5. Ibid., *passim.*
6. M. G. Smith, *Affairs of Daura*, 422.
7. Whitaker, *Politics of Tradition*, 314.
8. James Coleman, *Nigeria: Background to Nationalism* (Berkeley and Los Angeles: University of California Press, 1958), 364.
9. B. J. Dudley, *Parties and Politics in Northern Nigeria* (London: Frank Cass, 1968), 152.
10. Daily Times (Lagos: December 14, 1963), in Ibid., 116.
11. NEPU, *Sawaba Declaration of Principles* (Jos: Baseco Press, 1950), in Whitaker, *Politics of Tradition*, 35–39.
12. Whitaker, *Politics of Tradition*, 394.
13. D. J. Muffet distinguishes between "deference" and "acquiescence" as conceivable postures toward political rulers in Hausaland (and, by implication, elsewhere as well). Acquiescence may have the appearance of deference, but lacks some of the "intangibles" of deference that make political obedience legitimate. Some of these "intangibles" that Muffet cites are loyalty, custom, decorous behavior, perceptions of propriety, decency, seemliness, and manliness. A leader (particularly a "modern" leader) can propagate his rule bereft of such deference indicators for an indefinite period of time. Unless he creates new and sufficient opportunities for either key classes or the masses, however, he cannot rule without the spectre of overthrow— overthrow in the name of traditional legitimacy— hanging over him. See D. J. Muffet, "Legitimacy and Deference in a Tradition Oriented Society," *African Studies Review* 18 (1963).
14. A number of other variations of the story persist. Here, the simplest version is offered. See M. G. Smith, *Affairs of Daura*, for other permutations.
15. Whitaker ranked Daura as thirty-fourth in "traditional imperial ranking," out of a total of forty-three Northern emirates. See Whitaker, *Politics of Tradition*, 296–97.
16. William Miles, "Self-Identity, Ethnic Affinity and National Consciousness: An Example from Rural Hausaland," *Ethnic and Racial Studies* 9 (1986).
17. M. G. Smith, *Affairs of Daura*, 353.
18. Ibid., 348, 423.
19. Ibid., 351.
20. The 1959 elections were the first ones during which there was general, direct voting throughout the entire North.
21. M. G. Smith, *Affairs of Daura*, 350.
22. Kenneth Post, *The Nigerian Federal Election of 1959* (London: Oxford University Press, 1963), 13n.
23. Ibid., Appendix D.
24. Lugard deliberately chose an area that was not solidly Hausa, so as not to unduly antagonize or disenfranchise the non-Hausa peoples of the North.
25. Unfortunately, an adequate consideration of Kano politics, or even of their full impact on Daura, cannot be undertaken here. But see John Paden's *Religion and Political Culture in Kano* (Berkeley: University of California Press, 1973).
26. Whitaker, *Politics of Tradition*, 351.
27. Although personally familiar with the worldwide heralding of J. F. K. many years after his death, the author was struck, nevertheless, to discover, in

1983, a resident of Yardaji who himself had admired, and greatly regretted the death of, "*Shugaban Kendee.*"

28. C. S. Whitaker, "Second Beginnings: The New Political Framework," *Perspectives on the Second Republic of Nigeria* (Waltham, Mass.: Crossroads Press, 1981), 2.

29. See Richard Joseph, "The Ethnic Trap: Notes on the Nigerian Campaign and Elections, 1978-79," in C. S. Whitaker, ed., *Perspectives.*

30. Ibid., 17.

31. "The new framework of democracy that was put in motion cannot be said to have been primarily the product of pressures to emulate Western experience. On the contrary, the greatest significance of . . . the new Constitution . . . is that [its] primary point of historic reference is Nigerian experience. Furthermore, [it] bear[s] an imprimatur of broad, tentative, Nigerian approval. These were more important influences than the American model." Whitaker, *Politics of Tradition,* 7. Richard Joseph expressed a similar sentiment as discussant to the author's Africa Research Program seminar at Harvard University on December 12, 1984.

32. The fifty-member (all male) Constitutional Drafting Committee was composed of "'learned men in disciplines considered to have direct relevance to Constitution-making, namely— history, law, economics and other social sciences, especially political science. . . .' Not less than 50 percent of the members were either academics or university administrators." Oyeleye Oyediran, ed., *The Nigerian 1979 Elections* (London: MacMillan, 1981), 10.

CHAPTER 3: THE PARTIES: NIGERIA

1. Oyediran, *Nigerian Elections,* 16.

2. L. Jinadu, "The Federal Electoral Commission," in Oyediran, *Nigerian Elections,* 32-33.

3. Toyin Falola and Julius Ihonvbere, *The Rise and Fall of Nigeria's Second Republic: 1979-84* (London: Zed Books, 1985), 52.

4. L. Anise, "Political Parties and Election Manifestos," in Oyediran, *Nigerian Elections,* 69.

5. Ibid., 87.

6. Falola and Ihonvbere, *Rise and Fall,* 53.

7. Ibid., 53-54.

8. Ibid., 55; Anise, in Oyediran, *Nigerian Elections,* 79.

9. Anise, in Oyediran, 75.

10. Ibid., 84.

11. Falola and Ihonvbere, *Rise and Fall,* 56.

12. Ibid., 48.

13. Anise, in Oyediran, *Nigerian Elections,* 88.

14. M. Alabi, ed., *Elections 1983* (Nigeria: *Daily Times*), 106.

15. Ibid., 107.

CHAPTER 4: THE PARTIES: YARDAJI

1. The Shagari regime had indeed officially moved the Nigerian capital from the congested, southern port city of Lagos to a new location in the middle of the country. Geographically, though, Abuja is no more "Northern" than "southern"; yet it is significant that Northerners would see it as such.

CHAPTER 5: THE SKEPTICS

1. *SANARWA BAMASO; Matsan Yardaje Basa Ra'ayin Wata Jam'iyar Siyasa, Gaba Daya. Saboda Haka Mun Gaji da "Gafarasa." Bamu Ga Kahoba. In Mutun ki Gani Aiko Ya Ji a Duba Da Kyau. Karka Shigo, Saboda haka wanan Abu Ba na Mutum daya bane. Na Kowa da Kowa ne, In Kunne Ya Ji, Jiki Ya Tsira.*
2. "Letter That Began the Kano rioting," *West Africa* 3338 (July 20, 1981): 1633–34.
3. Diamond, "Nigeria in Search of Democracy," 910.

CHAPTER 6: ELECTORAL POLITICS IN HAUSA GARB

1. A. H. M. Kirk-Greene, *Mutumin Kirkii: The Concept of the Good Man in Hausa*, Third Annual Hans Wolff Memorial Lecture (Bloomington: Indiana University, 1974), 5.
2. Polly Hill, *Rural Hausa: A Village and a Setting* (Cambridge: Cambridge University Press, 1972), 29.
3. Kirk-Greene, *Mutumin*, 11.
4. Ibid., 9.
5. The English word has been incorporated into the Hausa.
6. M. G. Smith, "The Hausa System of Social Status," *Africa* 19 (1959): 247–48; "The Hausa of Northern Nigeria," in J. Gibbs, ed., *People of Africa* (New York: Holt, Rinehart and Winston, 1965), 134–35; M. G. Smith, *Affairs of Daura*, 41–42.
7. M. G. Smith, "Hausa of Northern Nigeria," 139.
8. Plato, *The Republic* VIII: 6 (Harmondsworth: Penguin, 1955), 330–31.

CHAPTER 7: CAMPAIGN RALLIES

1. M. G. Smith, in his Introduction to Mary Smith, *Baba of Karo: A Woman of the Muslim Hausa* (New Haven: Yale University Press, 1981), 27.

CHAPTER 8: SONGS OF INSULT

1. Attahiru I, sultan of Sokoto, in *Wakar Annasara*, quoted in Ibrahim Yaro Yahaya, "Oral Art and Socialisation Process," Ph.D. diss., Ahmadu Bello University (1979): 184.
2. Sa'ad Zungur, *Wakokin (Zaria, Nigeria, 1960), quoted in G. O. Olusanya, "Political Awakening in the North: A Re-Interpretation," Journal of the Historical Society of Nigeria* 4 (1967): 134.
3. Zungur, in Olusanya, 130.
4. This tendency could already be discerned in First Republic campaigning as Dudley's (1968) appendix of NPC and NEPU campaign songs attests.

CHAPTER 9: CHIEFS AND THE CAMPAIGN

1. This is not to say that the Nigerian military has been, or is, antitradition, or antichiefs. In fact, the military has generally recognized the role that the chieftaincy may play as a legitimate intermediary between government and the people, and as an institution of culture, religion, and morality. The point has been to limit the chieftaincy to this role and away from active, autonomous power-wielding.

CHAPTER 10: VOTING IN THE BUSH

In Anglophone Africa, the term "bush" is used — by Africans themselves — to designate "countryside" or "rural areas." (In Francophone countries, the equivalent is *la brousse*.) For ordinary Africans, "the bush" does not carry the negative connotation that the term may be construed to have in the west (such as in "bush league," to characterize a second-rate baseball club). This difference in usage reflects a less prejudiced approach to the rural-urban dichotomy than often exists in the west. In keeping with the spirit of the book, this apt African colloquialism is retained.

1. The central government deliberately chose the police to oversee the elections, confining the more potentially volatile military to their barracks during the election period.
2. "The voter [shall] . . . fold up the ballot paper and insert it in an envelope and seal the envelope and come out from the compartment and in the full view of the presiding officer and all others present, deposit the envelope containing his vote in the ballot box; have the space between a finger nail and the flesh of the finger marked with indelible ink and forthwith leave the polling station." *General Elections 1983, Directions for the Guidance of the Voters in Voting.*
3. Personal communication of Dr. Larry Diamond.
4. At least until this researcher, violating his normal policy of neutral noninterference, drew the wandering voter to the attention of the polling agents.
5. Including the then political affairs consul of the U.S. Embassy in Lagos.

6. The prospect of nighttime vote tallying in unelectrified areas posed a potential problem throughout many parts of Nigeria.

CHAPTER 11: THE RESULTS

1. State Department briefing for Fulbright lecturers and researchers, Lagos, 1983.
2. It is interesting to note the use of the word *ilmi*, which in context means "secular," or "modern," education; thus, the ability to commit electoral fraud was associated in the minds of villagers with the skills acquired at western (as opposed to Koranic, or religious) style schools.
3. This in no way implies that the chief himself was in any way responsible for the events that followed.
4. New bills are highly valued, for paper currency circulating in the village is usually in various stages of decomposition.
5. In Hausa, these were called *kurʼa na kauye*—bush ballots.

CHAPTER 12: THE COUP

1. Three and a half months before the actual coup, an NPP candidate (born and bred in Yardaji) who had lost his election bid (because of alleged rigging) made the following graphic prediction on how Nigeria's experiment with democracy would end:

> It will take place in the mosque, during Friday prayers. Someone standing behind the president will have concealed in his *babban riga* [the traditional long, flowing gown of the Northern Muslim] a pistol. The motions of prayer will begin: *Allahu Akabar*. Then, when everyone is bowing from the standing position, he need only reach into his gown, draw the gun, and shoot the President. *An gama* [And it will be all over].

As is well known, in terms of detail the prediction was inaccurate: President Shagari was not assassinated. Yet it is striking that, without any acknowledgment of inconsistency or irony, the bloody prediction was made in such a religious context (e.g., the mosque, Friday prayers).

Yet upon reflection, it is not all that outrageous. If politics in Northern Nigeria may in general be explained and understood through the paradigm of Islam (as Paden argues in *Religion and Political Culture in Kano*), then why should it be disturbing to imagine the ultimate political revolt taking place in a religious context as well?

POSTSCRIPT

1. As this book was going to press, Babangida had just announced that plans for a return to civilian government were being pushed back to 1992. At the same time, the Nigerian leader declared that no more than two parties

would be permitted in the next electoral system. See James Brooke, "Nigeria Leader Details Plan For Return of Civilian Rule," *New York Times*, July 2, 1987, p. A3.

2. Interview with Alhaji Muhammadu Bashar, emir of Daura, September 11, 1986.

3. Kenneth Post, *The Nigerian Federal Election of 1959* (London: Oxford University Press, 1963), 434.

Bibliography

ABUBAKAR, Sa'ad (1974). "The Emirate-Type of Government in the Sokoto
    Caliphate." *Journal of the Historical Society of Nigeria* 7.
ACHEBE, Chinua (1966). *A Man of the People.* London: Heinemann.
ALABI, Mac, ed. (1983). *Elections 1983.* Nigeria: *Daily Times.*
ALUKO, T. M. (1970). *Chief the Honourable Minister.* London: Heinemann.
BIAGHERE, Sunny (1984). "Buhari Woos the Obas and Emirs." *Africa Now,*
    March.
CHAZAN, Naomi (1979). "African Voters at the Polls: A Reexamination of the
    Role of Elections in African Politics." *The Journal of Commonwealth
    and Comparative Politics* 17.
—— (1982). "The New Politics of Participation in Tropical Africa."
    Comparative Politics 14.
COLEMAN, James (1958). *Nigeria: Background to Nationalism.* Berkeley and
    Los Angeles: University of California Press.
Constitution of the Federal Republic of Nigeria, with the Amendments (1979).
    Nigeria: *Daily Times.*
CROWDER, Michael (1962). *A Short History of Nigeria.* New York: Praeger.
—— (1964). "Indirect Rule—French and British Style." *Africa* 34.
—— (1968). *West Africa Under Colonial Rule.* Evanston: Northwestern
    University Press.
CROWDER, Michael, and Obaro IKIME, eds. (1970). *West African Chiefs: Their
    Changing Status Under Colonial Rule and Independence.* New York:
    Africa Publishing Corporation.
DIAMOND, Larry (1983). "A Tarnished Victory for the NPN?" *Africa Report* 28,
    November–December.
—— (1984a). "The Coup and the Future." *Africa Report* 28, March–April.
—— (1984b). "Nigeria in Search of Democracy." *Foreign Affairs* 62.
—— (1987a). "Issues in the Constitutional Design of a Third Nigerian
    Republic." *African Affairs* 86.
—— (1987b). "Nigeria Between Dictatorship and Democracy." *Current History*
    86.

—— (1988). *Nigeria in Search of Democracy*. Boulder: Lynne Rienner.

DRAKE, St. Clair (1965). "Traditional Authority and Social Action in Former British West Africa." In Pierre L. van den Berghe, ed., *Africa: Social Problems of Change and Conflict*. San Francisco: Chandler Publishing Co.

DUDLEY, B. J. (1968). *Parties and Politics in Northern Nigeria*. London: Frank Cass.

FALOLA, Toyin, and Julius IHONVBERE (1985). *The Rise and Fall of Nigeria's Second Republic: 1979–84*. London: Zed Books.

FAULKINGHAM, Ralph (1970). "Political Support in a Hausa Village." Ph.D. diss., Michigan State University.

GOLDMAN, Minton (1974). "Nigeria: Political Change in a Multi-National Setting." In D. Schmitt, ed., *Dynamics of the Third World: Political and Social Change*. Cambridge, Mass: Winthrop Publishers.

HEUSSLER, Robert (1968a). *The British in Northern Nigeria*. London: Oxford University Press.

—— (1968b). "Indirect Rule in Northern Nigeria." *South Atlantic Quarterly* 47.

HILL, Polly (1972). *Rural Hausa: A Village and a Setting*. Cambridge: Cambridge University Press.

—— (1977). *Population, Prosperity and Poverty: Rural Kano 1900 and 1970*. Cambridge: Cambridge University Press.

—— (1982). *Dry Grain Farming Families. Hausaland (Nigeria) and Karnataka (India) compared*. Cambridge: Cambridge University Press.

HISKETT, Mervyn (1973). *The Sword of Truth: The Life and Times of the Shehu Usuman Dan Fodio*. Oxford: Oxford University Press.

IKIME, Obaro (1968). "Reconsidering Indirect Rule: The Nigerian Example." *Journal of the Historical Society of Nigeria* 4.

JOSEPH, Richard (1981). "The Ethnic Trap: Notes on the Nigerian Campaign and Elections, 1978–79." In C. S. Whitaker, ed., *Perspectives on the Second Republic of Nigeria*. Waltham, Mass: Crossroads Press.

—— (1983). "Class, State, and Prebendal Politics in Nigeria." *The Journal of Commonwealth and Comparative Politics* 3.

—— (1984). "The Overthrow of Nigeria's Second Republic." *Current History* 83.

KIRK-GREENE, A. H. M. (1965). "Bureaucratic Cadres in a Traditional Milieu." In J. Coleman, ed., *Education and Political Development*. Princeton: Princeton University Press.

—— (1974). *Mutumin Kirkii: The Concept of the Good Man in Hausa*. Third Annual Hans Wolff Memorial Lecture. Bloomington: Indiana University.

—— ,ed. (1965). *The Principles of Native Administration in Nigeria*. London: Oxford University Press.

LAST, Murray (1970), "Aspects of Administration and Dissent in Hausaland." *Africa* 40.

LEVINE, Robert (1966). *Dreams and Deeds: Achievement Motivation in Nigeria*. Chicago and London: University of Chicago Press.

LUBECK, Paul (1981). "Islamic Networks and Urban Capitalism: An Instance of Articulation from Northern Nigeria." *Cahiers d'Etudes Africaines* 21.

—— (1985). "Islamic Protest Under Semi-Industrial Capitalism: 'Yan Tatsine Explained." *Africa* 55.

MACKINTOSH, John (1966). *Nigerian Government and Politics*. London: Allen and Unwin.

MAIR, Lucy (1958). "African Chiefs Today." *Africa* 28.

MILES, William (1986a). *Elections and Ethnicity in French Martinique: A Paradox in Paradise.* New York: Praeger.

—— (1986b). "Self-Identity, Ethnic Affinity and National Consciousness: An Example from Rural Hausaland." *Ethnic and Racial Studies* 9.

—— (1986c). "Islam and Development in the Western Sahel: Engine or Brake?" *Journal. Institute of Muslim Minority Affairs* 7.

—— (forthcoming). "Partitioned Royalty: The Evolution of Hausa Chiefs in Niger and Nigeria." *Journal of Modern African Studies.*

MILLER, Norman (1968). "The Political Survival of Traditional Leadership." *Journal of Modern African Studies* 6.

MINER, Horace (1965). "Urban Influences on the Rural Hausa." In Hilda Kuper, ed., *Urbanization and Migration in West Africa.* Berkeley: University of California Press.

MUFFET, D. J. (1975). "Legitimacy and Deference in a Tradition Oriented Society: Observations Arising from an Examination of Some Aspects of a Case Study Associated with the Abdication of the Emir of Kano in 1963." *African Studies Review* 18.

NICOLAS, Guy (1984). "Métamorphose de l'Islam Nigérian." *Le Mois en Afrique* 223-224, 225-226.

OJIAKO, James (1981). *Nigeria: Yesterday, Today, And . . .?* Onitsha: Africana Educational.

OJIGBO, Okion (1980). *Nigeria Returns to Civilian Rule.* Lagos: Tokion.

OKOLI, Enukora (1982). "Revolution or Tradition in Kano?" *West Africa,* January 4.

OLA, R. O. F., and C. A. OLOWU (1977). "Recent Administrative Developments in Nigeria." *Quarterly Journal of Administration* 11.

OLOFSON, Harold (1976). "*Yawon Dandi:* a Hausa Category of Migration." *Africa* 46.

OLUSANYA, G. O. (1967). "Political Awakening in the North: A Re-Interpretation." *Journal of the Historical Society of Nigeria* 4.

OREWA, G. O. (1978). "The Role of Traditional Rulers in Administration." *Quarterly Journal of Administration* 12.

OYEDIRAN, Oyeleye, ed. (1981). *The Nigerian 1979 Elections.* London: MacMillan.

PADEN, John (1970). "Aspects of Emirship in Kano." In Michael Crowder and Obaro Ikime, eds., *West African Chiefs: Their Changing Status Under Colonial Rule and Independence.* New York: Africa Publishing Corporation.

—— (1973). *Religion and Political Culture in Kano.* Berkeley: University of California Press.

—— (1981). "Islamic Political Culture and Constitutional Change in Nigeria." In C. S. Whitaker, ed., *Perspectives on the Second Republic of Nigeria.* Waltham, Mass: Crossroads Press.

PEIL, Margaret (1976). *Nigerian Politics: The People's View.* London: Cassell.

POST, Kenneth (1963). *The Nigerian Federal Election of 1959: Politics and Administration in the Developing Political System.* London: Oxford University Press.

POST, Kenneth, and Michael VICKERS (1973). *Structure and Conflict in Nigeria, 1960-1966.* Madison: University of Wisconsin Press.

REED, Cyrus (1982). *The Role of Traditional Rulers in Elective Politics in Nigeria*. Fifth Annual Graduate Student Paper Competition. Bloomington: Indiana University.

ROBINSON, Pearl (1983). "Traditional Clientage and Political Change in a Hausa Community." In Pearl Robinson and Elliott Skinner, eds., *Transformation and Resiliency in Africa*. Washington, D.C.: Howard University Press.

SANI, Habibu (1977). "Traditional Rulers and Local Government." In Suleimanu Kumo and Abubakar Aliyu, eds., *Issues in the Nigerian Draft Constitution*. Zaria: Baraka Press.

SMITH, Abdullahi (1970). "Some Considerations Relating to the Formation of States in Hausaland." *Journal of the Historical Society of Nigeria* 5.

SMITH, Brian (1967). "The Evolution of Local Government in Nigeria." *Journal of Administration Overseas* 6.

SMITH, Brian and G.S. OWOJAIYE (1981). "Constitutional, Legal and Political Problems of Local Government in Nigeria." *Public Administration and Development* 1.

SMITH, H. F. C. (1961). "A Neglected Theme of West African History: The Islamic Revolution of the 19th Century." *Journal of the Historical Society of Nigeria* 2.

SMITH, Mary (1981). *Baba of Karo: A Woman of the Muslim Hausa*. New Haven: Yale University Press.

SMITH, M. G. (1959). "The Hausa System of Social Status." *Africa* 19.

—— (1960). *Government in Zazzau: 1800-1950*. New York: Oxford University Press.

—— (1964). "Historical and Cultural Conditions of Political Corruption Among the Hausa." *Comparative Studies in Society and History* 6.

—— (1965). "The Hausa of Northern Nigeria." In J. Gibbs, ed., *Peoples of Africa*. New York: Holt, Rinehart and Winston.

—— (1978). *The Affairs of Daura: History and Change in a Hausa State, 1800-1958*. Berkeley: University of California Press.

SMYTHE, Hugh, and Mabel SMYTHE (1960). *The New Nigerian Elite*. Stanford: Stanford University Press.

WHITAKER, C. S., Jr. (1967). "A Dysrhythmic Process of Political Change." *World Politics* 19.

—— (1970). *The Politics of Tradition: Continuity and Change in Northern Nigeria, 1946-1966*. Princeton: Princeton University Press.

—— (1981). "Second Beginnings: The New Political Framework." In C. S. Whitaker, ed., *Perspectives on the Second Republic of Nigeria*. Waltham, Mass: Crossroads Press.

WISEMAN, John (1979). "Structural and Ideological Tensions in a Rural Hausa Village." *African Studies Review* 22.

YAHAYA, Ibrahim Yaro (1979). "Oral Art and Socialisation Process." Ph. D. diss., Ahmadu Bello University.

Index